To my very good friend
Gorman Dix

Tales of
Monterey
...and More

Irv C. Rogers

PARK PLACE
PUBLICATIONS

Published by
Park Place Publications
Pacific Grove, California
www.parkplacepublications.com

ISBN: 978-1-943887-05-7

Printed in U.S.A.

First U.S. Edition: October 2015

BOOKS BY IRV C. ROGERS

Motoo Eetee, Shipwrecked at the Edge of the World

Tales of Monterey . . . and More

DEDICATION

Helyn

Judie

Susan

Erik

CONTENTS

.

PREFACE

The Weekend Pass

In January 1951 the Korean War was into its seventh month, and I had passed my twenty-second birthday by six months. There was no surprise when I received a card in the mail inviting me to join in the military training offered young men at Fort Ord, California and there to be rousted out of my bunk very early to witness the Monterey Bay mornings. I had read Steinbeck's description of them in his Cannery Row as "the time of the pearl," so while on the base I could enjoy each one in all its damp, literary glory.

At Fort Ord many valuable facts were to be learned viz: #1. There is a critical difference between the right foot and the left foot as one proceeds across the parade ground. #2. A man can subsist indefinitely on a strict diet of powdered eggs and dehydrated potatoes. #3. The drill instructor will turn you into a fine soldier if you scrub the barracks floor with a small brush and lye soap every Friday night. #4. After you pull the pin from a grenade, be sure to dispose of it quickly; the grenade not the pin. #5. Lastly, always take advantage of a weekend pass whenever available.

The weekend pass was the few hours granted a soldier to go to town and see men with hair still on their heads and people not dressed in olive drab. Monterey was my choice to visit as I had never enjoyed the big cities. I attended movies and wandered about the streets happily stepping over cigarette butts I wasn't instantly ordered to pick up. One day I meandered onto Wharf Number One.

It was still a working wharf then. Purse seiners backed in to hoist their heavy nets into the big tanning tanks there. The nets came out brown after the treatment that preserved them. Market fish was hoisted from the smaller boats and taken into the shops to be gutted and displayed on beds of ice.

I was feeling a bit peckish and asked a local for a good restaurant. I was directed to one close by decorated in what might be called the cubist style or maybe it was the manner of another avant-garde art movement. Over the door was the name "Angelo's."

The baked fish was good and the view was good.

I went to the cash register to pay my tab and there tending it was a girl with dark, Italian eyes. Very nice. The thought came to me instantly and I asked, "You want to go to a movie?" The offer was accepted. Always take the weekend pass. You never know what will come to pass.

The next day I went to meet her parents, Filippo and Rosina. In later days and weeks I was introduced to her brothers: Angelo, Tony, Toto, Georgie, John, Andrew and sisters: Anita, Agatha, Mary, Josephine, and Jennie. There were their spouses too which doubled the number I met. I suspected she was related to half of Monterey when she named a list of the grandchildren.

Emilia, the girl with the dark, Italian eyes determined the course of my life for more than sixty years.

NONNA

The residents of the portion of Monterey that slopes up the hill from Pacific Street to High Street came in good part from Italy and settled there in the thirties and forties, coeval with the sardine bonanza. Since that time many have died and many have moved away, yet enough of them and their children remain there to keep the local wits referring to that part of the town as Spaghetti Hill, a phrase always spoken and received with good humor. In the earlier years fishermen living there could walk down Franklin Street and be at the wharf in a few minutes no auto required; so it followed many of them chose to live in the neighborhood. At one time nearly half the houses there were stuccoed, painted, and trimmed in pastel shades of blue, pink, and aqua. A parapet wall or an entryway roof can still be seen topped with a smattering of tile. That tile along with the favored colors gave a faux Mediterranean flavor to Spaghetti Hill, and from a distance on the low ground to the east or from a boat on the bay the houses resembled variously colored boxes tiered on the hillside. One of the houses up on Monroe

Street was not painted any of those sunny hues but a leather brown; and could it be described in many ways, as a home, a headquarters, or the seat of a local clan.

Filippo and his wife Rosina, and at times, many of their children lived in that house. Rosina's mother also lived in their house or perhaps more accurately was inherent in it. She was never called by her given name, Maria, but was always referred to as Nonna. Another woman, widowed and childless, had been welcomed into the home; and for years she helped around the house and was named godmother to many children. For assiduously filling that office she was simply known as Comare.

Fillipo and his wife had raised their six boys and six girls to adulthood and had seen them all married. In the decades of the fifties and sixties they were repeatedly made grandparents at close intervals. The house was still thought of as a home by the children and grandchildren regardless of their age and the size of their families. If they were within driving distance, presence there on Sunday dinner was a tradition that was honored if there were no other commitments. On Christmas it was almost obligatory. Everyone entered the house by the back entrance that was the preferred, direct route to the kitchen; and the banging of the old screen door announced each new arrival.

Rosina's pasta-plumped figure stood before the

kitchen stove on Sundays; and there she measured salt, pouring it from a one pound box into her hand, then scattered it into the water boiling in a four-gallon kettle. She returned the salt to the pantry and came out with a five-pound package of spaghetti. The spaghetti, snapped in half, was scattered into the water with one hand, and with the other hand she stirred the kettle with a large, wooden spoon.

That spoon was not always used as a cooking implement. In earlier years it was also used to correct the young daughters when they misbehaved. A humorous recollection shared among them even decades later was that they had all "survived the wooden spoon."

Steam rolled up from the pots on the stove. The water bubbled; the sound seemingly paced the chatter of the people in the room. Steam from the large kettle on the stove rose to the ceiling and crossed over to the outside wall. There it descended and condensed on the glass of the tall north windows until several beads of water started on crooked downward paths. They increased speed and changed direction as they met and fused with the next drop below. Scents of garlic and oregano lingered in the warm, humid air. Rosina cooked pounds of spaghetti, penne, or rigatoni every Sunday knowing it would all be eaten. There was no guessing how many of her children, in-laws, and grandchildren would arrive to eat; but pasta, sauce, bread, and salad were easily adjustable to any number in a few minutes. Sunday dinners were well attended and there was never an empty chair at the large kitchen table. To find seats some of the family moved to eat in the dinning room, a space normally considered a tad formal. The women seated at one side of the kitchen all talked at once. Toto, his brothers, and the other men of the family sat around the table and passed their judgments on the players of the NFL.

Between these two camps a parade of children of all ages passed back and forth asking for drinks or tugging at mother, sister, or brother. The teenagers, bound for some place not yet agreed upon, hurried out the back door.

Rosina ignored them all and fished out a few strands of spaghetti from the kettle and placed them on a saucer. She crossed to the table and presented the saucer and a fork to Filippo. To test the readiness of the spaghetti, he cut it with the fork. Then he tasted the pieces with a smack of the lips. His head dipped in a quick nod to Rosina. That was his approval. The meal could be served.

Toto and I were called to lift the kettle off the stove. We carried it to the sink and poured its contents into a big colander. A cloud of steam rolled upward obscuring the entire sink and drain board. We had to wait for it to rise to see well enough to finish the job. The spaghetti was divided into two large bowls, and the sauce that had been simmering since morning was added to them.

The dinner began with the passing of baskets of fresh Italian bread and bowls filled with pasta. From my seat at the opposite end of the table from Filippo, I watched a hand reach across the table for a salt shaker. A pair of hands broke away slices of bread nearly cut from the loaf. Single hands rolled forks over and over to ball up the spaghetti and move it from bowl to mouth. Some proffered side dishes, glasses of wine, grated cheese. Some paused in the air awaiting requested items. Certain hands moved, poised, and moved again in artful descriptions of the spoken words.

The meal ended and most of the women gathered in the dinning room inevitably talking of babies and pregnancy and changing diapers when cries indicated the need.

Filippo remained in his reserved place at the head of the table peeling an orange and only half-listened to the men arguing about which of the ballplayers were the greats and who were the bums though he never understood the least of their reasons.

All the latecomers arrived and had their meal. Nonna seeing there were no more of the family to be blessed with her near-toothless smile turned and walked toward the entryway, a small room at the front of the house. She paced slowly from the kitchen, resonant with loud chatter, and entered the pantry. Her hair, white and wispy, was gathered just above the nape of her neck in a small bun; but some wisps always escaped the pins and stuck out in protest to confinement. Her bowed figure, barrel-shaped and covered with a full print apron, was outlined by light from the dining room windows ahead. She shuffled forward with her left hand touching the edge of the sink or the pantry wall for balance or perhaps just from habit. Once in the well-windowed entryway, she settled into her painted wicker chair with its arms stained with hand oil and the seat dished by her weight.

The children were on their own after finishing their meal and squealed and chased after each other in the driveway, the yard, and even out in the street, playing with an urgency that edged toward a passion.

Nonna watched them hanging gibbon-like on the pipe railings around the yard, and when the play became too rough she stood up and knocked on a pane of the French doors. "Eh! Eh!" she warned, tapping her temple. "You breaka dees, you die!" But it had no effect. She would add something in Italian and lean forward with her plump nose almost touching the glass. The children could hardly make out the English words through the panes and knowing almost no Italian might pause only a second with a puzzled look on their faces. Nonna was resigned to being ignored. Her age had not granted her leave to be outspoken, to be the matriarch, the arbiter of morals and taste, or an even partner in a conversation. When she advanced an opinion in the crowded kitchen, people waved her words aside. "She is old," someone would say excusing the interruption with a shake of the head, "Yes, very old and she doesn't speak English. She knows nothing of such things." Nonna would pull her elbows close to her sides and hold her hands on her lap. In silence and with a quick hunching of her shoulders, she excused herself for presuming to speak. Then she might catch someone's eye and holding a shaky finger to her lips open her damp eyes to their widest in a biting appraisal of the whole affair.

From her wicker chair she was witness to all that happened on Monroe Street: the breakdown of cars, the passage of children to and from school, the sales at the side of the vegetable peddler's truck. She took in all the talk around her and noted it in her memory. She caught the drift of spoken English though she could only respond with few words of that language accented by the rules and rhythm of her native speech.

There were windows in the south wall, and just below the level of their sills was a wicker table with its top crowded with potted plants: African violets, coleuses, and azaleas. Some of the containers were still wrapped in bright, anodized foil hinting of their origins as gifts. Each day Nonna poked the soil with a finger to test its moisture and pinched off dying leaves and spent blossoms. That busied her for a few minutes. Having done her gardening she eased her bulk back into her chair. The sun room was her place.

The house was built on a lot six feet higher than the sidewalk, and from that height Nonna had a good view of the street a block in either direction. From there she had watched the years pass in Monterey. On weekdays she waited for the postman until he came into view striding along the along the sidewalk. She timed her rising from the chair and opened the door just as he reached the landing at the top of the steps. Nonna took the mail from his hand and placed it on the dining room table to be sorted and handed out to the intended recipients.

In some way by some misunderstanding she believed the circulars and advertisements were about science. Since it was known I was much interested in things scientific, she began handing me a wad of junk mail everyday. It was easier to accept them than to explain their true purpose; thus I read about momentous car sales and low interest loans. If she received her Italian newspaper, she immediately read the serialized romance and made half-audible comments as if the characters in the story were flesh and blood and the action was taking place that moment somewhere in the world.

One Sunday she sat in her wicker chair as usual and looked out of the French doors. The view except for one or two new apartment buildings on the lower side of the street was the same as it had been for years. The shore of the bay swept around to the east, then north. Off to the southeast Jack's Peak, covered with dark pines, appeared little different than it had to Vizcaino, the first explorer who discovered the bay three centuries earlier.

Nonna looked up and gave a wide, eye-wrinkling smile as I entered the room. "Allo," she greeted me and motioned for me to sit on the hassock. We sat quietly enjoying the warmth of the sun and the view toward the bay.

Nonna's hands fidgeted over the arms of her chair. From the corner of my eye, I saw her steal a sidling look at me; but I didn't acknowledge it. Her mouth was held in a sagging O to ease the labor of her breathing.

"The war comin-a," she said abruptly.

"What?" I asked, looking at her.

Her wet eyes stared at me. She held up her right index finger and slowly pronounced the words, "War-a-one. War-a-one."

I thought for a few seconds...what was she trying to say to me? "World War One?" I asked.

"Si, si," she replied eagerly. "*Mi figlio* Antonio, say he want to go. Want to fight. 'No, no,' I say."

"But he went anyway?" I said, making an easy guess.

"Si, si, he go," she continued. "The war comin-a bad. Antonio gone a longa time."

I recalled my sketchy history of the First World War. Caporetto, Isonzo…Italy's battles with Austria had been disastrous.

"*Giornale* say many die. I pray and-a pray." Nonna looked ahead, mumbled in Italian, and dipped her clasped hands up and down to add a physical effort to her words. After crossing herself she turned and said, "Letter come from-a *ospedale. La gamba* … you know." She held her open hands above her right knee as if displaying it. She stared at me, waiting for me to comprehend.

"His leg?" I asked.

"*Si, si, malato.* Oh comin-a bad."

She pressed her palms together again and nodded her head in time with the syllables of her prayer. Then she opened her hands and held them up before her in supplication. The wattles of flesh under her chin shook with the intensity of her speech. I pieced out what I suspected was the story of her son. He had been sent back from the front after suffering a leg wound. It had become infected or gangrenous.

"I pray…every day I pray," Nonna said, gripping my arm with an unexpected strength.

A mental picture came to me of her walking a street

of Marsala to the nearby church were she shuffled into its dimmed interior, lit a candle, and by its glow and that of other guttering candles asked for the intercession of the Virgin. I guessed at that time Antonio was lying in a military hospital hot with fever or growing rigid with tetanus.

Nonna held up one hand, palm out, and let out two breathy words, "*Aspettare ... aspettare.*" She rose from her chair and shuffled into the parlor and down the hall.

She returned in less than a minute, dissolving my images of a suffering Antonio. She held something in her hands that resembled a plate. "Antonio die," she announced settling into her chair and cradling the object in her lap.

It was plaque of some sort about seven inches in diameter. On the lower two-thirds of its glazed surface was a line drawing of a woman in a filmy gown drawing herself from a stormy sea onto the base of a massive stone cross placed providently at hand. From the top of the cross, rays of light beamed down onto her face. Apparently she was the sole survivor of a vessel foundering in the distance. Across the top of the plaque was a spray of blood-red roses. Except for the petals of the blossoms the illustration was rendered in sepia over a buff background making the plaque to appear old; but the color of the roses was fresh and had an uncanny, liquid shine. I was compelled to touch the flowers to prove they had not been painted only a few minutes before. In the upper third of the plaque, just to the left of its center, an oval space had been provided. Its size and position just balanced the picture of the woman and the cross below. Photographic emulsion had been applied to the oval and a picture of a young man from the chest up developed on it. Around his neck was the stand-up collar of an old style uniform. He looked surprised as if he had not expected the clicking of the shutter. The photograph lacked the fine gradations and crisp blacks of modern black and white film.

I watched Nonna's hands tremble as she held the plaque. They were covered with thin, slightly transparent skin; and on their backs were colonies of irregular brown spots.

One of her fingers pointed to the oval, and then her hand moved out and gripped my wrist. "Mi figlio, Antonio," she breathed.

I heard someone enter the room behind me and turned to see who it was. Ellena, one of the neighbors, was standing there. She spotted the plaque in Nonna's lap.

"Oh, is she telling that story again?" she asked.

Nonna, caught at it again, rose from her chair and carried the plaque back to her room.

"I wish she wouldn't repeat it," Ellena complained.

"She gets so upset and tells it in the same way every time...never varies a word. If you stay here very long you'll hear it again. Scusa, I have to see Rosina." She nodded and headed back to the dining room.

Nonna returned and settled herself into her seat again. She propped her right elbow on the arm of the chair and leaned her head against her cupped hand. She lifted her left hand head-high for a moment, then let it fall limply in her lap. Her rheumy eyes stared at the view through the French doors to Monroe Street and the roofs of the houses lower on Spaghetti Hill.

On most weekends Nonna's remaining son Andrew came to visit for an hour and brought little gifts of candy and pocket money. In a day or two she had parceled it all out to the grandchildren. That was what it was for: the candy for them to eat and the money to spend and make smiles on little faces. Andrew's visits were breaks in the passage of time. He sat with her in the sunny little room and talked and made jokes. His face always broke into a broad grin after each pun or parody.

The familial resemblance between Nonna and her son was obvious. Both had a full face and large ears. The notable difference was their voices. Nonna's was uneven and labored due to her age. Andrew, though, spoke every word with confidence and an orator's sense of effect. Even when sitting in the large kitchen, the volume of his speech was a shade more than was needed.

Nonna was weakened by the accumulated ailments of age. Her movements required more effort. She paced slowly through the rooms always touching the door frames and walls with her fingers lightly as she passed. She spent the late night hours dozing in an upholstered chair. Eventually she wakened, struggled to her feet, and found her way down the hall to the bedroom.

Each morning as Nonna rose from her bed she saw the photograph of Antonio on the plaque. It was propped up on the dresser amid the scent bottles and holy figurines. Despite his youth, his face showed all the characteristics of the family. It was the ever-present reminder that he had suffered the less than heroic death of a soldier in a war that made little sense. It had been and remained forever the ultimate sorrow.

FILIPPO

If you knew Filippo the least bit, you could spot him
blocks away walking up Franklin Street to his house.
He wore his cap low on his head covering most of his
gray-white hair and kept his hands in his pockets while
he paced tirelessly up the hill in short strides. He wasn't
quite five feet tall and appeared even shorter dressed in
his usual thick flannel shirt and baggy Frisco jeans.

At home he always sat at the end of the kitchen table
with his chair backed up to the fully opened pantry door.
In many years I had never seen that door closed even
partially; it was always fully open. In the narrow space
remaining between it and the wall a jug of red wine was
kept, the source and vintage of which I never learned. The
jug was at least half-full or more whenever he reached
back and brought it out at mealtime to fill many glasses,
and it was replenished at sometime by some person
unseen. The concealed door knob held a long hank of gill
net which Filippo repaired when he had spare moments.
If there were no visitors sitting at the table, he would
move the loop of the mesh onto the visible knob and
with his wooden oogia or "needle," loaded with twine,

replace all the parts of the gill net which were broken.

"You no wear a cap?" he asked the morning he had invited me to go out fishing.

"No, I don't have one," I replied.

"Ah, you need a cap," he warned. "Make-a cold deesa morning. I get one."

He went into his bedroom and returned with a cap that except for the color was a a mate to his. He slipped it onto my head at a cockeyed angle and then declared, "Now, you fisherman. Whadda you say?"

With his son Toto we were to lay out a setline in the bay and pull it up again. Filippo had brewed strong coffee, and we took a few minutes at that early hour to drink a cup for the ocean air was expected to be damp and cold and the hot fluid was a hedge against it at least for the first hour.

While I sipped my drink, I pulled my borrowed cap off and looked it over. In the 1930's and 40's all of us boys had called them golfers' caps since every picture of a golfer we had seen was wearing one. The loose round top was made of pie-shaped pieces sewn together. All the apexes met in the center under a cloth-covered button. The top lay flat on the head with the some of the fullness pulled forward over the bill. For most of the first half of the Twentieth Century it was the badge of the workingman and those defined by Lenin to be the proletariat. It was also the headgear of sportsmen and schoolboys. Proportions varied, but its appearance remained much the same whether it was used for casual wear or for sports. I pulled my cap back onto my head and wondered if it made me look like some victim of the Great Depression recorded in a grainy Movietone newsreel.

Toto wore a knit navy watch cap over his dark, curly hair and stared across the table with dreamy eyes thinking, I presumed, of the day's catch.

A cigarette hung from Filippo's lips and the smoke from it twisted upward causing his eyes to squint at times. His forehead was pale contrasting with the lower half of his tanned face. He always wore his cap when making a new net in the backyard and during the hours spent out on the ocean. All his smiles and frowns ones never faint or halfhearted were recorded in the many seams in his face as if they were cut in fine grained wood.

We finished our coffee and left the kitchen quietly by the back door. No one else in the house was yet awake. We climbed into Toto's car, drove to Fisherman's Wharf, and found the place illuminated by the first gray morning light wherein there was not a soul yet stirring. It would be hours before the first tourists wandered out of their motel rooms and into the shops and restaurants then opened. Shadows were ill-defined and graded out into the lighted portions of objects. A lone gull, a sentry on a guano-ed roof, turned a lackluster eye on us and deciding his bailiwick was safe from the three flightless creatures below gazed seaward again.

Filippo unlocked the shed and I helped him move the fuel tank, outboard engine, fish boxes, boots, and life jackets out to the electric hoist. Toto was rowing the skiff from its mooring spot around to our side of the wharf where he would tie it up to a piling below. From the walk-in freezer Filippo brought out two dish-shaped baskets about two feet in diameter. Each one held coils of the wiry setlines with hooks and leaders hitched to them a fathom apart. On each basket there were about a hundred hooks baited with a morsel of squid and arraigned to dangled in a thick, gelatinous border around its rim. They had been prepared the day before. All of the equipment had to be lowered into the boat by the growling hoist and stowed in its proper place. We placed fish boxes just forward of the thwart and the set lines aft of it. The life jackets were tossed into the bow, and the fuel tank was pushed into a corner of the transom. Toto mounted the engine and unhitched the bow and stern painters. On the second pull of the starter rope the engine buzzed. He engaged the clutch; and the skiff started forward sending a bow wave to each side that rolled away all the squiggling, multicolored reflections on the water. As we rounded the end of the wharf, I looked back and saw the first bluish puff of smoke that had shot from the engine was still hanging in the air over the tarn-like water of the bay. From the end of Wharf Number Two, the notes of the big bell mounted there rang out and echoed back from around the harbor. That resonant toll would be our guide if the fog closed in. Once passed the end of the breakwater, the skiff began rising and falling on the swells from the northwest. Our course was along the rocky coast of New Monterey.

The sardine canneries had been built there overlooking the breaking waves. Some were so close water surged around their pilings at full tide. In fog or at night when they could only be partially seen, the high walls gave the impression a castle had been sited at the shore where assault would be difficult. These walls though were not of stone or any such durable material but were framed up of battens and siding in the cheapest possible manner. There were no sardines any more at least in any quantity that would make it pay to run the canning lines again; thus the buildings were neglected. Salt-ladden air had rusted away the heads of the nails and the wind had worried a few boards loose until they flapped with each gust. Wood surfaces had been dashed by years of rain until paint flaked off. On the clear days some oblique rays of the sun highlighted every detail of grain, split, and knot. Glazing putty in the windows had cracked and peeled away allowing some of the panes of glass to fall and shatter on the rocks below. The canneries were a fitting monument to human greed. Seventy, eighty years before, the sardines could be taken by stretching a net in the surf. When the days of those handy bonanzas were over, purse seiners were employed; and they followed the fish in ever widening circles until they reached the limit of their population.

Filippo and his sons had purchased one of the big boats just before the collapse of the industry. The boat had to be given up, and all but one of the sons went into other businesses. Only Toto and his father fished with the setlines and gill nets for the local market. I suspected it was not so much to make money but more from long habit and the wish to be useful that Filippo went out on the bay on cold mornings. He was not be one to sit with other old fishermen and bemoan the decline of fishing and the rise of the tourist business. To fill out the days with games of Bocce ball and gossip would be neglecting a man's duty while there were fish yet to be caught.

Toto stood astride the tiller arm and with his knees guided the skiff along the ironbound coast. Filippo changed from his shoes to boots and put on a brown, rubberized apron. He switched places with Toto and held the tiller while his son went through the ritual of changing. The engine buzzed steadily and drove the skiff sled-like over the low swells. Filippo watched the rocks passing by a hundred yards away.

We were off the site of the Old Chinese Village. There was nothing left of the old jackleg shacks not a board or window frame. It had burned one night decades ago; some say suspiciously. It would have taken little to set the thin walls ablaze, an upset kerosene lamp or an arsonist's match. In the soil overlying the granite shore there was certainly a layer of ash and charcoal. Embedded in it there might be broken dishes, bits of iron, melted glass, and artifacts that would take much study to explain. The Chinese there had specialized in taking and drying abalone for the Asian market. Their boats were of Asian mold that they launched off the rocks.

The old photos recorded a haphazard yet oddly harmonious and fitting collection of shanties, drying racks, lean-tos, and poles that comprised the village; but in its day the accretion of unpainted lumber was counted an eyesore by those of chamber of commerce thinking. The men who had inhabited it had worn the queue that reached to the waist at their backs or even lower. Their costume was little different from that of fishermen on the coasts of China.

Filippo watched the shore for landmarks that would guide him to his favored spot to lay his lines. Once satisfied he was over the rocks and in the kelp that was the haunt of the cod and other market fish, he gave a nod to Toto. His son cut the throttle back and disengaged the clutch. Filippo tossed the weight and the pole with its float and faded red flag over the side. Toto engaged the clutch again and the engine idled in gear holding a little tension on the setline as his father let it pass over the side through his short, thick fingers. He had to watch that no loop twisted up in the hard-laid line that would foul the hooks.

On we went to the west slowly easing the line over the side until we had set it for a quarter mile or more across the rocks below. Fish, nice big ones, we hoped were darting in to swallow the gobbets of squid on the hooks.

"Now we go back and pull up," Toto announced and swung the skiff around toward our starting point. At the flag Filippo reached into the water and pulled up the end of the setline. It was laid athwart the boat; and as the line was drawn up on one side and the fish removed it was re-baited and dropped back into the water on the opposite side of the boat to rest again on the bottom and catch more. One by one fish were unhooked and pitched into the box. Not every hook had a catch or even bait remaining on it. Some of them had been nibbled clean by little fry or crabs. One had snagged an octopus. Its tentacles twisted around Filippo's arm as he disengaged the hook. Once he had it free he placed it on the thwart and bashed it with the backside of the gaff. It went limp as a sodden rag and Filippo tossed it into the box with the rest of the catch. The line began to resist the pull to the surface. Soon it was running straight from the gunnel to the bottom. It was "up and down" as sailors used to say when a ship's anchor was about to be broken out of the ground.

"Kelp?" I asked.

"No, Rocks. It's snagged on the rocks," Toto explained.

"Here make like-a dees," Filippo said and positioned himself at the gunnel. He wrapped the line twice around his hand and began pulling. His face contorted and he grunted with the great effort. The gunnel of the skiff dipped until there was only three inches of wood above the surface of the water. I moved to the other side to balance the boat. Suddenly the line came loose. The hook had straightened out enough to allow it to break free. Filippo resumed taking the fish off the hooks and Toto baited them again. We had gone another fifty yards when I saw an arm of the octopus slowly slither out of the box and reach over the gunnel. The animal was half out of the skiff when Filippo seized its body, pulled it to his mouth, and gave it a fierce bite. Again it went limp and never showed the least sign of life after that. We completed harvesting the fish and replacing the bits of squid. On the second pass the line was cleaned of catch and not re-baited but coiled in the baskets. The box was half full of our catch. Toto revved up the engine and turned the bow toward the end of the breakwater.

Water was sloshing about in the bottom of the skiff, and to be useful I picked up the old olive oil can that served for a bailer and began dipping water over the side. I crouched and scooped up the gill suckers and small bits of seaweed with the water. As I tipped the can over the side little streams piddled from rust holes in its bottom.

The boat had been painted many times, and parts of some layers were worn away where boots abraded the paint on the bottom. There was evidence of a blue, green, brick red, gray, even a pink coat. On the sides and in the corners the paint had peeled off in odd patches creating an atlas of imaginary kingdoms.

At the hoist we raised and unloaded the fish and all the equipment. Everything was stored away in its usual place. Toto sorted the fish into different boxes and loaded them onto a hand truck. Filippo and I walked along with him as he wheeled the catch to the fish market forty yards up the wharf from the shed.

"Ah Pop, I gotta freezer full of this stuff," The market man complained. "Why don't you go after reds. I could sell them easy."

"I bring red, then you wanna ling. What I got you no want," Filippo replied. "These-a fresh fish, Joe. Not like yours all soft and stink."

'You know this business ain't what it used to be," Joe said. "Remember how all the women used to walk down here to the wharf and buy nice, fresh fish two or three days a week. Now they all live outta town and drive to the supermarket and buy little pieces wrapped in plastic. Who knows how old it is or what it is? Next month the rent's goin' up. Gee, I don't know why I stay in this business. It's all goin' downhill."

Toto stared at the ceiling of the shop ignoring the shop man's complaints. Filippo busied himself with rolling down his wet sleeves.

"You know," Joe explained, "you guys got it easy. You go out for a couple of hours and you're done. You can go home. Me, I gotta get ice. Gut and fillet. Get the tables in shape. I have to be here all day long." Joe leaned over our boxes and poked at Filippo's catch. He eyed them as if they were only fit for fertilizer; but then he bought them all for the going price, knowing they had not been out of the water an hour and a half.

We drove back up the hill to Filippo's house, parked the car in the driveway, and entered the kitchen by the back door. The women were now up. All the lights were on, and the coffeepot was on the stove perking a new batch. We were greeted by Rosina who then directed me toward the table. Filippo went to his chair at the head of it. Nonna raised a hand in welcome and as always gave us her smile, one best mustered by one from the Old Country

Next to her sat Comare. She smiled too but couldn't match Nonna's version which mobilized the entire face.

There was a cozier feel to the kitchen now. It was warm and filled with the aromas of brewing coffee and the simmering sauce of tomatoes, garlic, and oregano.

"Ah," Filippo said, raising his head a little and sniffing, "Rosina make a sauce. Verra good. You come and eat-a dees afternoon. You like pasta.?" He gave a quick nod cueing me to sit.

Rosina carried in a platter of breakfast rolls from the pantry and placed it on the table. A minute later she brought full mugs of coffee for us.

I bit into my roll and enjoyed the sugar icing. My body needed the nourishment. The coffee was hot, and its warmth flowed into my stomach as I carefully sipped it. The Bay water was eternally cold, and the short time spent out in the skiff had chilled my blood even through layers of good wool. We finished our rolls in silence. Now and then the women exchanged a few words in Italian. Having finished my coffee, I rose from my chair to leave. "I have to go now," I said.

"But you'll be back to eat about one o'clock?" Toto asked.

"Sure, he come back," Filippo broke in. "He know Rosina cook *molto bene*." Filippo pinched his thumb and forefinger together at the corner of his mouth and turned them as if he were twisting the tip of a moustache. He clicked his tongue and winked at me. "Ah, vera good. You like," he assured me.

When I returned to the house that afternoon, the kitchen was full of people who had arrived to eat.

We finished the salad, bread, and rigatoni; and the women removed the empty dishes. They placed bowls of apples, oranges, and bananas in the center of the table. Paring knives were added and we set to at a slower pace quartering the apples and peeling oranges. The stout, full-aproned women returned once more with cups of coffee. The talk around the table slackened, and there was never any agreement as to the relative talent of the NFL players.

Filippo finished his coffee with a gulp and smiled widely at the people crowded around his table. He slapped the sides of his stomach and announced, "Ah, feela good now. Think I gonna live." He looked to my end of the table and asked, "How-a you? You eat-a OK?"

"I'm fine. Full up to here," I replied.

"Sure," he joked, "you eat-a. Maybe you gonna live too."

He leaned back in his chair and began to sing:

Vole un bacin d'amore

Il tu Federi

Chequello paghera

Suddenly he jumped from his chair and seized Rosina by the waist. He tried to dance with her, but she broke away and with reddening smile returned to the chore of clearing the table.

Filippo imitated the sound of street musicians. Tee da da, tee da da, tee da da, he sang in the 6/8 time of a tarantella. He hopped around, holding one arm behind his back and one arm over his head with a curving forefinger extended from his closed fist. All the chatter stopped. Everyone looked up, smiled, and watched the performance.

After a few bars he abandoned his dance and returned to his chair. We gave a round of applause and laughed at the surprise dance.

Slowly the talk started again on the women's side of the room.

"Eh, next a month I be marry fifty year," Filippo said to the men at the table. The women hearing those words fell silent and listened.

"I marry Rosina. I fisherman. Fifty year go, phit! I still fisherman. Whadda you say? Too longa time one woman? I get-a new wife, maybe. Get-a pretty one, OK? He smiled and looked us all for a reply. "No!" he answered his question, "New woman want-a dees, want-a dees. Eh, I think I keep-a dees one. OK?" He looked at Rosina and then to us and winked.

There was laughter again.

Filippo smiled and fingered in his shirt pocket for his Lucky Strikes. He found them and lit one.

The men and women left a few at a time over the next hour.

Toto, Filippo, and I were sill at the table when the last one said goodbye and went out the back door.

Rosina brought a letter and a pen and placed them on the table before Filippo. He slipped a card from the envelope and signed his name on it. The pen didn't move smoothly over the card as he pushed the point around, consciously drawing each letter in succession. He looked up and saw that I was watching his effort.

"I no write so good," he admitted. "I go-a school two, three day, no more. My family send me a school, but deesa profess' I no like. He no like-a me, so I go fish.

"One day profess' comin' a boat an' say, 'You go-a school now!' I just-a twelve year. I say, I no like-a you an' no like-a you school. Waste my time. I fish.

"'Ah,' he say, 'You comin' a school. I make. I gotta stick. I teach you.'

"I take bag a calamares, you know squid."

Filippo pantomimed how he reached down and grabbed the bag with his right hand.

"Now you sonnuva bitch, I say, I teach-a you. Whap! Right on-a face."

His fist was tense, grasping the imaginary sack of squid.

"Then I comin-a the other way. Whap! Bastard, I say. You teach-a me nothing. I teach-a you. I just-a twelve, no more, just-a twelve. He no come back. An' I go fish."

Filippo smiled. Then he looked at his hands placed palms down on the cool surface of the table. Slowly he flexed his short, thick fingers. He narrowed his eyes to bar the smoke lingering up from his cigarette.

I WILL FIND YOU

Suddenly the ritual of the Sunday dinner was broken. Rosina could no longer serve the mounds of steaming pasta, large bowls of salad, and half-cut loaves of soft, yeasty Italian bread. She had fallen ill with cancer and was confined to her bed. Finally she was taken to the hospital. The sons and daughters agreed that Nonna should move to Andrew's home and remain there until Rosina recovered. Andrew had made the preparations for his mother's arrival renting a hospital bed and engaging a nurse to stay with her while he worked.

The appointed day came when she was to leave for her son's home. Andrew arrived and had her packed bags loaded into the trunk of his big, white car.

Nonna had been told many times that she was to leave that day; but each time she had ignored those words hoping that some unforeseen event would keep her in her old bed at night and allow her to greet the mail man each morning. Part of the family was gathered at the front room entrance to the porch to say goodbye. Nonna avoided looking at them. She was not going to budge. She did not wish to go to a strange house where there were few known faces and no wicker chair and no sun porch that overlooked a street.

Andrew stepped forward and sat on the hassock that was always near the wall. Nonna turned away and pretended not to hear the pleas of her son and the others. Her eyes were focused on something beyond the French doors. "Nonna," Andrew asked, "you take care of me long-a time ago, Eh?"

Nonna gave a reluctant nod without turning her eyes toward him.

"You change my diapers and feed me with a spoon like this?" He mimed the feeding action with an imaginary spoon. "You remember," he resumed, "you remember when we had the store back in Boston?"

"Si, si," Nonna answered, showing some interest in what her son was saying.

"You sat in the corner and watched for the little boys stealing candy. They never saw you and were surprised when you caught them. You remember?"

Nonna nodded again and smiled.

There was a pause in the talk, and during the silence she could only stare through the glass of the doors. For twenty years the view of the town, the bay, and the hills had been nearly her entire world. She had watched it when it was partially obscured in fog or rain and when it was lighted by a brilliant sun at midday. The view was familiar even in its small details, and in old age familiar things were comforting.

"Now I take care of you," Andrew announced, "just like you take care of me. First I sing you a lullaby, the same one you sing me years ago. You know the words, eh? You remember how it goes? ... *Bo ... bo ... Dormi figlio e fai la nanna.*"

Nonna turned slowly to her son as she recognized the words of the song.

"Now what's next?" Andrew urged.

Breathlessly and almost without tune she sang, *"E se'to figlio."*

"Ah, you remember now," Andrew laughed and resumed the song, *"Non vuole dormire ..."*

Nonna joined in and they finished the verse together, *"Chi sa che pensiere deve avere, Bo, bo, bo, bo."*

As the song ended Nonna reached out and clasped Andrew's right hand with both of her hands. She moved them in a slow rising and dipping motion of a fervent prayer. Her eyes, always a little wet, were filled with tears. All those crowded into the porch and standing in the living room doorway watched without a word spoken.

Nonna looked up and knew that all those waiting there considered the move was for her good. Rosina now far too ill to take care of her was in the hospital. She also recognized that there was no other choice and gave a weary nod. She would grant her son's wish, get into the machine, and ride halfway around the bay to his house. She would rest in the strange mechanical bed and permit the nurse who spoke no Italian to take her pulse.

Andrew took one of her arms and I took the other to lift her to her feet. As we did so I felt the bone within the soft, loose flesh of her arm. We guided her out the door. At the first step she eased her right foot down, then the left foot down. Second step: right foot down, left foot down. Third step: right foot down, left foot down and continued slowly until we had descended all twelve steps and stood on the sidewalk. There we paused for a rest with her bowed figure between us. Bright sunlight penetrated her thin hair to the pale scalp.

By careful moves we worked her through the car door and onto the rear seat. Andrew's wife got in to help make her comfortable.

Everyone paraded down the steps and gathered at the car windows to say their goodbyes.

"I no come back," Nonna declared in reply to them all.

"What are you saying?" someone protested. "You will be back when Rosina is well. Andrew will bring you back."

Nonna would not listen to their words and negated them with a shake of her head and the upraised palm of her right hand.

There were renewed promises that she would return to her sun porch, but she ignored them and spoke a word of Italian to Andrew. The car started, rolled along Monroe Street, and turned left at Franklin.

Two weeks later I arrived at the brown, shake-sided house at mid morning. The driveway was full of cars and more were parked at the curb on both sides of the street. Most were recognizable as cars of the family.

At the kitchen door I met the familiar aroma compounded of oregano, garlic, and fish. The room was full of people. Filippo and Toto had gone fishing as usual but were now sitting at the table in their work clothes. Filippo sat in his chair at the end. In the center of the table were several shot glasses and a half empty bottle of bourbon. Every seat was occupied. Most of the men sat at the table. Others fetched more chairs and sat with the women around the walls of the room.

Andrew sat with one leg cocked up on the other knee and fingered an empty shot glass in his hand. His large face was flushed and his eyes were reddened.

Filippo poured a shot of whiskey and slid it toward me with a solemn nod that I should drink up.

Andrew began to speak, "Mama, I say, it's past eleven o'clock. We better get to sleep. She say nothing, like she was thinking for a while. She fiddle with her rosary and then look at me. 'Ah,' she says, 'I will go to bed now, but I will not wake in the morning.' Eh, Mama, how you talk, I say. It was like she make a joke. And then she ask, 'How are my granddaughters?' Fine, I say, justa fine. 'Here take-a these things from my pocket and give them to Rosina,' she say. It was silly little things she collect. Look this handkerchief with the rose in the corner. Some string and a piece of candle. I took them and she went to sleep. Then maybe two or three o'clock this morning I hear like she was talking to somebody, but nobody answer. 'I'm comin-a,' she say. '*Aspettare*. When I am ready, I will find you.' It make no sense. It's a dream I think and go back to sleep."

Andrew heaved a sigh and waved a hand in the air. "Such a quiet there was in the house this morning," he said in that voice a shade louder that the size of the room required. "It was so still, it-a wake me. You get used to some noise and when its-a gone…eh, you can't-a sleep.

"Eh what can you do? She was an old woman. We all gonna die some day."

Andrew wiped his left hand across his eyes with a quick motion.

When we arrived at the church there was already a crowd there divided into two groups that faced each other across the walkway that led from the street to the doors of the old San Carlos church. In the years when

Nonna and her family arrived in Monterey it was a close community where most recognized others about town. Faces were now heavier and the lines in them deeper. Heads of hair were grayer and thinning.

One of the bells in the tower swung on its yoke sending its heavy, reverberating notes over the streets, houses, and El Estero Lake. The hearse rolled to a stop at the curb and the practiced attendants stepped out and opened its rear doors. Six of Nonna's grandsons, all the sons of Rosina and Filippo, lifted the casket and bore it to the entrance of the Royal Chapel. They halted just within the weather-beaten doors and placed the burden on a dolly. There it rested to receive the blessing of the priest. After the last swing of the censer and the last sign of the cross was drawn in the air, the casket was rolled along the aisle toward the altar.

The narrow interior of the Chapel filled quickly with people and the noises they created: clicking footsteps, sporadic coughs, and whispered messages.

The Mass began. Words of Latin echoed down the nave past the Stations of the Cross to the loft where they were answered by falling notes of the Amen.

A multitude of details met the senses: the bright colors and gilt on the holy figures, the intoning voice of the priest, and the smells of wool clothing, hot wax, and mothballs.

The wavering flames of the candles seemed to detach from the wicks and float in the darkened interior. A faint, amber ambiance surrounded them as if they shone through a fogged window.

Everything ran together to form an unsorted impression of the rite.

"When I am ready, I will find you," Nonna had spoken in the middle of the night. She could only have been speaking to Antonio, to the last image of him she had known, the one on the plaque. He had posed stiffly in his new uniform for the photo, and the standup collar seemingly held him to attention. He had gone into battle like multitudes of other young men vaguely thinking it would be a short war in which most casualties would be on the enemy's side. But he and his comrades were betrayed in hopeless, uphill battles. The war ground on. Disaster followed disaster. The politicians could not break free of their vaunting, past oratory, admit error, and end the war.

The flames returned to their wicks, people stirred in their pews. The mass had ended and the casket was being rolled down the aisle. As it passed by I saw hemispheres of the Holy water clinging to its glossy plum-colored surface. Each bead condensed the light from a stained glass window and reflected it as a single point.

On the way out of the Chapel I was handed a Holy

card. A color gravure picture of Joseph holding the Christ child was on the face of it. At Joseph's elbow was the corner of a workbench on which lay a wood plane and a square of archaic design. Around the two figures was a thicket of leafy roses which faded into a hazy background. On the reverse side of the card was the prayer of Saint Francis that began:

> Lord make me an instrument of your peace
> Where there is hatred let me sew love
> Where there is injury...pardon
> Where there is doubt...faith

Above those words and in a different type and blacker ink were the name and dates:

Mary Pavia

1869–1966

We walked out into the bright light under a half-clouded sky. The traffic moved rapidly on the streets, and a jet plane whined overhead to make a landing at the airport a mile and a half away. Nothing appeared to have changed, but we all remembered the empty wicker chair just behind glass panes of a French door on Spaghetti Hill.

SERENDIPITY IN THE VENTANA

Hﾟigh clouds had insinuated across the sky all afternoon, and it became a mite colder as sunset neared. Breaths of air stirring between the Ponderosa pines loosened a few trifling flecks of snow and sent them turning slowly right and left until they touched lightly on the ground. I knelt at the base of one old tree to tie off one end of my tarp. It wasn't the best shelter to use in midwinter backpacking in the Ventana Wilderness; but if the coated nylon were tied to convenient rocks, logs, or whatever objects offered, it would fend off rain. There were times the lash-up had kept me dry when others had suffered wet sleeping bags in tents.

A pair of juncos flitted out of a Manzanita bush and landed ten feet away on the mat of pine needles not covered with snow. Their small, black heads cocked to the right and left to bring each eye to bear on the hiding places of insects and crannies where seeds might have fallen. They picked and probed with practiced ease and must have found tidbits for their bodies were round and their feathers sleek. No tumid, juicy caterpillars were to be found in that season; yet the spunky style of the two creatures assured me that they would forage a living. Each one flashed an eye at me every few seconds to monitor my intentions. They worked the litter close to my shelter, but let me know I was not one to be trusted. During the night while I was cosseted in goose down and nylon, those two fluffed their feathers and slept in their Manzanita roost. It might rain or snow all night, but they would be out at daylight working their turf.

In the morning campers steeped their freeze-dried nourishment in boiled spring water and watched the juncos extract their food from the slope and contend with another cold day in the pine forest.

Six of us rolled up our gear and made an early start from the camp located just below the crest of a ridge. We moved up along a trail which appeared to be at the top of the world for the ground sloped away to each side from the rocky path and the horizon was a distant circle of morning haze.

We had traveled only a few hundred yards when the first rays of the sun broke in the east and back-lighted the condensing breaths of those ahead laden with big packs. They, in an odd way, resembled steam locomotives puffing around the turns of the path ahead. Snaps and D rings of my pack squeaked at each stride, and the weight of the food and equipment against the back felt reassuring in the chill air. To be in the familiar harness again and pacing along a new trail was reassurance: the good life was still on.

Ahead a sapling pine came into view, one with an odd, inexplicable sparkle about it though the air was a near dead calm. When nearing it we saw that a freezing rain had coated each separate needle. The ice sheaths were glass-clear and the dawn light had glinted from their facets as we paced toward it. There had been no disappointment. Each trip into the Wilderness yielded some image or some event that drew our minds out of the channels of day to day life.

The Ventana Wilderness is a handy place twenty miles south of Monterey. Its location in the National Forest and its geography make it easily accessible to the people of the county. Within an hour or two they can be parked at a road head and changed into their vibram-soled clodhoppers. Whatever enticed them, air scented with sage and pine, a black dome of sky filled with stars, the alternating calls of owls at night, or campfire mate-ship they find it all without driving to some distant mountain range. They savor thoughts of such things along the trail as they adjust the straps and hip belts of their packs.

The word, wilderness, engenders images of forests, rivers, mountains, or deserts and also denotes the absence of humanity and human artifacts. There is also a connotation of expanse, but the Ventana is a mere cluster of ridges between private holdings on the Coast Highway and the Salinas Valley. It is a fragment of wilderness with a few foxes, deer, cougars, and bears; and with no great breadth it is difficult to find a campsite in it that is more than a day's hike from a road head. A trip for several days requires sitting in one or two camps or taking oddly plotted routes and loops.

A steep, jagged ridge separates the Big Sur and Little Sur water sheds; and on a topographic map its contour lines are squiggly and pinched together indicating a steep and rumpled mass of rock and earth. When seen from the north or south it is a barrier seemingly cast up to prevent passage, one far more effective than Hadrian's construction and one at an least equal to the Great Wall. In the middle of this ridge, on its crest, is a rectangular notch twice as high as it is wide. Its sides are nearly vertical as if the rock had been quarried away. The sill between them can be seen as floor-flat after one of the wild fires has burned out the trees and brush. Thus it is a window in the barrier, albeit without the top crosspiece. This window, or "ventana" in Spanish, gave its name to the nearby peaks and to the Ventana Wild area that was created in 1929. In later years the Wild Area was enlarged and became the Ventana Wilderness. There have been additions since then and the Wilderness extends for 34 miles from Mount Carmel to Kirk Creek. Before the Wilderness was created, there were in-holdings and access roads. Little cabins were nudged up to creeks. Some of the cabins have been dismantled and some were swaybacked by the constant pull of gravity and then collapsed from the added effects of dry rot and termites. The roads to them have been gullied by rain and blanketed by the steady fall of leaf and needle, and their outlines can barely be detected and traced around the contour of the land.

In the narrow valleys that empty their streams onto the tumbled rocks of the coast, massive redwoods shade the creeks and their banks creating a damp, semi-lighted world of mosses, ferns, and sorrels. Heavy rains of winter weaken the soil and any Sequoia leaning too far to one side and poorly rooted crashes to earth and lies canted on the slopes. It might remain rooted enough to allow a branch to continue to grow at an angle from the parent trunk giving the tree a prospective, tenuous second life. Mosses, bright green in the wet season, slowly spread over the dead trunks; and after lying for decades in its moist covering the wood rots and crumbles to a rich soil for the next generation. Few flowers bloom under the coastal redwoods: some small white ones, some irises and violas, and perhaps a lily in a sunny opening. A slug a half-foot long, a banana in name and color, eases over the litter seemly brighter by contrast to its dull surroundings.

Toadstools of the same hue push up through the layers of composting litter once the rains begin, but the dominant colors are the browns of tree trunks and fallen needles and the greens of ferns and seedling redwoods. The trails through the lower canyons pass around the great columnar Sequoias, and there treading boots are silent on the spongy duff. It is an enclosed place, shadowed, muffled by the height and mass of the trees. Any smoke from campfires hangs in the air, trapped between the long sloping limbs of the redwoods. There is little wind that penetrates to move the smoke or make the least soughing in the forest.

Roots of the creek-side trees have fingered their way into the packed soil and gravel and hold it against the rush of high water, but in heavy rains currents have swept around bends and scoured cavities into the banks. The roots that were forced into gnarly, twisted networks between boulders and bedrock are exposed, bruised, and splintered by stream-driven rocks. Along sections of the banks, mythmakers and their believers might find detailed scenes for a fantasy wherein they might imagine kelpies and kobolds peeking from undercut banks and from openings between rocks lifted or split by swelling roots. Beyond the edges of the streams clumps of dead grass and driftwood are caught up in the bushes, proof of the height of water during the winter spates.

In the years of heavy rainfall, tree trunks several feet in diameter are rushed seaward, battering whatever they meet. The ebbing stream then leaves them stranded on worn, rounded boulders or half buried in gravel. Detours must be made where the hulks have blocked the trail. Climbing over the grounded boles with a top-heavy pack is awkward at best so the better choices are to break a way through the brush or splash through the creek.

After decades of winter rains some logs might reach the ocean and be cast back onto the rocks and sand with their sharp angles and projections battered away and their color weathered to a soft gray. The sea currents often carried some along the coasts to Southern California and there Chumash Indians split the huge gifts of the winter and built their canoes or "tomols." The Channel Islands were then within their reach.

Raging, episodic fires have left charred patches on some of the trunks and a few are burned hollow for part of their length. Their condition is part of the repetition of growth and destruction in the forest.

There is a shy bird which can be approached quietly but never too closely when it is perched on rocks near the streams. There is no mistaking the drab-colored water ouzel for it moves with a syncopated rhythm dipping its body to an unheard beat of a Latin band. The movement has no apparent function other than to make the bird noticeable for if it remained still it would easily blend into the background of cobbles. From a rock or log it eyes the tumbling water for prey and then suddenly dives to the bottom. It uses its wings to propel itself in the dense medium and competes with fish and crawdads for worms and insects. Seconds later it pops up onto a stone and continues its dance: chic-a-chic-a-boom-chic.

Summer is hot in the higher parts of the Ventana inland. Beyond the reach of the fog and marine air, its hard work to pound up the exposed trails. Smaller streams diminish, dry up. The last rains end leaving the chaparral sere and easily ignited, a very real danger. In the warmer months a cloud of midges will gather a few inches from the faces of hikers and remain at that distance whether they march on or rest. They are not the most vexing of the bugs, but a few might be inhaled while panting up a long trail. Mosquitoes and biting flies are far more bothersome. They surely sense that flushed, perspiring faces contain much rich blood. Repellants must lose their potency or the insects become inured to it for they attack by scores in the heat of the day. Fortunately the evening air cools their ardor and campers are given a little peace around their campfires. During the hot season some hikers and campers keep to the lower valleys for the shade and the assured water supply, though even there they also suffer from annoying insects.

From late fall to early spring it is far more pleasant to trek up the switchbacks to camps 2000 and 3000 feet above the coast road. As a bonus the trails are deserted in the coldest weather, and it is rare to meet more than a few backpackers seven or eight miles from the road head.

Winter is the time to keep to the high country and enjoy a wider sky. Farther up the coastal valleys the Sequoias diminish in number and yield space to tanoaks, alders, bays, and maples with wider openings which admit more sunlight. The warmth, the airiness, and the rustle of those trees are preferable to the winter dampness and half-light of the canyons below. The high routes pass through stands of black oak, madrone, and pine, and across treeless, grassy balds. The hiker following these paths in the fall is sometimes favored with cool, blustery winds that whip leaves from the trees and drift them along the ground. The last ones clinging to the branches of the oaks are translucent and the light passing through them reflects from the litter on the ground. It is pale gold in the air beneath wide branching limbs. The trunks of the trees and striding hikers are rendered in an ambient, faintly yellowed illumination, or so it might be imagined. Leaves continue to fall until they are more than ankle deep. Kicking and crunching through their abundance is one of the anticipated pleasures of the season. The rite of autumn, the suspension of growth, and the tuning of the earth to the coming cold is to be celebrated and meditated. Winter makes an incongruous change on the open mountainsides. The first rains soak into the dry earth and in two or three weeks tender grasses arise. The scent of those growing blades and stems, sweet and soporific on warm sunny afternoons, is carried along the ridges. Any gusts of wind that strikes the balds spreads waves in the grass, bowing and lifting across the slope. It all seems a little odd if there are patches of snow from the last storm extant in shaded pockets.

Local and repeat backpackers favor certain camps with views of peaks and valleys or the ocean. Once they have set up their tents and fluffed their sleeping bags, they wander out where the last of the sun can be seen. Below them the slopes are losing their details in shadows while the trees about and their camps are in the last rays grazing the camber of the earth. From the high trails ridge after ridge can be see finely edging the pale, lower sky.

For thousands of human lifetimes the rain has fallen in the Ventana, tumbled the redwood boles and granite boulders, and washed sand to the sea. In all that time only the minor details of the land have been changed by the weather. But the Ventana didn't escaped the effects of human presence. At the edges of the Wilderness there have been repeated attempts to turn rock and trees into cash. Before the highway was constructed along the coast, tan bark was stripped from oaks and dolomite rock burned to make lime. The products could only be loaded onto small steamers or barges to take them to their markets. Logging was more successful and there are great stumps in the western canyons still bearing the notches cut in them for the axmen's footboards. Those infringements didn't reach far inland. It was the ruggedness of the mountains, lack of more valuable minerals, and scattered nature of the usable trees which allowed the Wilderness to be established there.

There were a few who attempted homesteading, but the plowable land was in small patches scattered along a rugged and roadless coast. All supplies had to be brought in by coastal steamers and then packed into the interior on mountain trails. Independence came at a high price.

The Ventana Wilderness is there because it couldn't be turned readily into money.

Overhead at 25,000 feet Jets rumble and leave their swelling ribbons of vapor across a clear sky; and balloons, escapees from car lots, lose helium and settle onto the brush. All the while the little black-headed juncos teach their lessons of persistence and optimism in the manzanita.

The Ventana is a reminder that when there is no longer an Ultima Thule we will be living in a world circumscribed, known in all details, and purged of variety, and adventure. The pelting rain, the hoarfrost on the dry ferns, and the looping descents of spent leaves are the reality outside the dulling of cocoon of condos, cars, and shopping malls.

EL CAMPO SANTO

If you stand in or near the old cemetery, El Campo Santo in Monterey, and listen to the traffic on Fremont Street it is a constant rumble accented with the snarl of horns and the bark of motorcycles accelerating to full speed. A good guess is that most drivers in the vehicles on that street are traveling to earn salaries and commissions. El Campo Santo had once been the quiet spot located on a tongue of land surrounded by the U shaped El Estero Lake. There are countless places like El Campo Santo where bird calls, the low of a cow, or bark of a dog were once the few sounds heard; but now they suffer the constant noises of the auto, the most convenient and inefficient of transports.

On any workday, during working hours the traffic passing over the Pearl Street bridge is constant; and at noon time a few vehicles that pass over the Lake turn off and stop on the bare strips of earth on the north and west side of the old cemetery. There are usually one or two route trucks or delivery vans that pull in, but most are cars that stop there. The nine to five workers who drive them park in the shade and settle back to eat their fast food lunches done up in paper with corporate logos or munch on the contents of a brown bag packed at home. Their eating is slow-paced, perhaps affected by the comparative quiet of the place. Long, asymmetrical limbs of Cypresses shadow the ground on the west side of the cemetery. On the northern border there are tall eucalyptus trees with trunks four and five feet in diameter. The drivers manage to park with at least the forward part of their vehicles in some shade.

In the morning the lake is smooth and ducks and coots calmly draw vees across its surface. As the day progresses the northwest wind picks up, ripples the water; and the light of the sun is returned from its surface in rhythmic flickerings.

After their lunches are consumed, some of the drivers sit listening to the news on the radio or nodding to the beat of a rock band. Others lean back against their headrests and yield to a nap with a fragmented dream.

Only a few yards away just beyond the black iron fence are rows of gravestones, and when viewed at low angle they appear to be nearly uncountable as trees in a forest. Stone stands behind stone in a perspective where they are crowded by a compression of distance.

There are sparse clues in the names and phrases carved in the marble and granite, and if more were known there would be tales of hates, loves, and the pride of people who lived good lives. If those parked there walked past the rows of markers might they imagine that beneath them were sailors, storekeepers, draymen, wives, blacksmiths, hookers, farmers, and horse thieves?

That ground beyond the black iron fence has been a cemetery for more than a century and a half and the third burial ground for the Presidio and Pueblo of Monterey. It was the consecrated ground for Catholics; but later a diseño, a plat, drawn about 1842 shows a line drawn from north to south dividing the peninsula into two equal halves. A quill-written phrase generously granted the eastern half (the farthest from the town) to Protestants and strangers to bury their dead. The cemetery was probably created in the early 1830's and considered at the time to be a sufficient distance from the Pueblo. The City of Monterey has long since grown around it, or more accurately leaped far beyond it. Noisy streets now surrounded the burial ground on every side.

A walk through El Campo Santo should begin at one of the northern gates beside the tall gum trees. On the damp and rainy days the trees give off the medicinal scent of their leaves and oily seed cases. Even a light breeze will rustle the leaf masses and create a murmuring. After passing the second or third rows of stones it becomes evident that there are not more than a half dozen styles of the modern markers. Perhaps the monument people are pushing certain ones or there is less desire to express individuality.

The older stones are more original, even fanciful. Some of the later ones do have one feature that sets them apart. By some process small photographs have been affixed to the stones. The pictures are protected under glass ovals and circles and except for the colored ones they seldom fade. Most are studio photos posed before the stock backgrounds provided. The men are dressed in rarely worn suits and the women are in formal dresses pinned with corsages. Thirtieth and fortieth wedding anniversaries were the most probable occasions for the poses. Fortunately there are some pictures that are simple snapshots. They record the deceased standing by a fence or a car or sitting at a table. Those photos were likely culled from family albums when it was discovered that there were no formal portraits. Most candid shots are of working people who didn't think a professional photograph was needed or affordable. The casual snaps disclose far more about their subjects in their once comfortable milieus: in their homes, at work, or at some picnic. They are revealing like the deceptively simple camera work of Walker Evans and give the savor of the person in the midst of living rather than a record of the end of a life. The older markers can be spotted between the newer blocks and slabs by making an unhurried walk along the paths. A Celtic cross of charcoal gray granite stands out against the white wall of the crypt next to it. Someone had wired a nosegay of plastic flowers to it perhaps two or three years earlier. The petals and leaves, brittled by the sun, have snapped off and fallen to the gravelly earth. All that now remains are the stems with a faded bit of green pigment in them. They are still held to the stone by the rusting wire that completely encircles the marker. It has been a long time since that act of remembrance was made, and the one who wired them there might now be interred somewhere in the same cemetery. There are even a few of the traditional wood crosses extant. Two have had their white paint renewed recently while others have suffered neglect and the weather and show only the slightest smudge of paint. Wood has a short life in the watered lawn, and some of the crosses attest to that appearing truncated as their rotted ends are reset. One cross having fallen was left leaning against the fissured bark of a cypress. The marker for one grave is a thin, weathered board set up in the ground with a cross fifteen or sixteen inches tall nailed to its top. The legend on the board is in black letters.

Near the western edge of the burying ground, under the thick limbs of a live oak, stands a slab of marble tinted green by a fine growth of algae. Its top end is a half circle like those of archetypal Halloween headstones. In the rounded half, a cross is incised. Below that is the legend:

> TH. Williamson
>
> Murdered in Monterey County
>
> 9th Nov 1855
>
> R I P

Williamson, a muleteer, and his partner Issac Wall were probably the innocent victims of the famous Roach-Belcher feud over the Sanchez treasure.

A few paces to the south of the Williamson grave is a larger, much fancier stone. Its style recalls the ornate tastes, even ostentation, of the Nineteenth Century; and its carved legend reads:

> Sacred
>
> to the memory of
>
> Maria
>
> wife of
>
> Alexander Raine
>
> Died in Castroville
>
> May 1, 1876
>
> aged 34y's
>
> 6m's & 17d's
>
> a native of County
>
> Rosscomon Ireland

The name Rosscomon has a significance that has been nudged farther into the background by the succeeding events of history, yet its import is not lessened the least by them. Famine was endemic to Ireland, and by 1846 that county and those to the west and south suffered the worst effects of the failure of the potato crop. Evicted families huddled in holes or wandered the roads, begged, ate grass, and died.

Maria would have been four years old then with the odds much against her survival, yet she had not ended her life as a pale corpse in a roadside ditch or died of the "black fever" in the workhouse. Somehow she reached this part of California (still rough and tumble in those decades) six thousand miles away and had another thirty years of life.

This woman would have no misunderstanding about her origin and hoped that all who read those lines learned that this daughter of Erin had lived through the great dying and the misery of the immigrant ships. To do so was an achievement, and it must have left her with never fading memories. There is sadness implicit in the few words carved on her stone. She knew she would lie forever in a distant land for time and distance and the famine had broken her link to Rosscomon.

One of the oddest memorials is a large slab of stone lying flat. "Munras y Familia" are the only words carved on its slick surface. Many of that family are buried beneath it, and their exact locations are no longer known. An all-inclusive marker serves well. The ones under it had a far different early childhood than that of Maria Raine. They had been born into a new and sparsely peopled country where food was plentiful and where land would not be divided and subdivided until it could hardly support a family. They didn't suffer any lurking fears. On this coast time passed in slow, unmarked progression from dry season to wet season. The bull and bear were matched in the ring. Bets were laid on the cockfights. Fiestas, fandangos were announced and well attended to break the monotony of nights and sunny days.

The older stones such as Maria's give the age of the deceased in years months and days. After reading the inscriptions something of their lives can be imagined. They lived for a shorter while than we, but not much less. It is when the ages of children are factored in that the life expectancy then becomes lower. Surviving before the Twentieth Century was a matter of luck and heritage. Childhood was a gauntlet of diphtheria, small pox, and fevers to be passed through before the young could enjoy adulthood. There are many small markers here topped with recumbent lambs or little crosses and a generation of lichens. Single ones are placed beside the larger stone of a parent while some others are gathered together in small colonies ringed with a curb. The death of the child and following sorrow took more from the parents than their long workdays or heavy labor.

Near the center of this cemetery there is a marker that is a puzzle. It is a square of unfinished sandstone a material not found nearby. It lies flat and measures about two feet in both dimensions. The stone's surface is a bare inch above the surrounding gravel and roots, and it has not been dressed or touched with a chisel except for some numerals that could only be taken for dates.

5/8 30

6/10 30

These markings might represent May 8 and June 10 or August 5 and October 6 in the year 1930. Was it a memorial for a child who had lived a month or two in the early Depression? The hard economic times could explain the material and the nature of the marker. Later, when on an errand in the county recorder's office I searched for the names of those who had been born and died on these dates. I found most of the birth certificates grouped around the first few days of the month. It was evident that the birth and death certificates had been accumulated and brought to the courthouse in batches. The 1930 file was a large one. Without the name the search could last hours. It was a "Catch 22." The name was what I wanted, the name of who was beneath that crude stone.

Except for the well off, everyone worked from first light to well after dark. Energy from fossil fuel had not spread beyond the use in the steam engine and hard labor was still part of the callings of most men. Their wives washed the soiled clothes by hand, sometimes in a tub of water heated over a wood fire. There were always chores to be done, meals to be cooked, the beds to be changed and made. When day work was finished, the sewing and mending were done by lamplight. The cotton clothing they wore was pressed with a flat iron heated on a coal or wood stove. It was a never-ending job to bring in fuel. Yet their pace of life was slower. Things didn't have to be completed at such a critical speed as today.

They died of consumption, tetanus, apoplexy, colic, and the pox. They suffered from some parasites and maladies that could be cured easily today by a simple prescription. Anyone who contracted a contagious disease was taken to a hospital of sorts. Among the waggish and cynical it was referred to as the pest house. Patients recovered with little effective help, or died and were quickly removed to the cemetery.

If the people that parked outside the fence were to get out of their cars and walk the lanes between the stones, reading the incised words as they went, would their small concerns seem less urgent? Would they see the names as a roll of people who had lived their lives and worked dutifully hard.

Near the end of the lunch hour the drivers start their cars and pull out into the flow of traffic. At one o'clock there are no more vehicles parked on the grassless earth near the black iron fence. Those who ate their lunches there are in the Twentieth-first Century rhythm of life, shuffling papers, tallying numbers, and delivering useful things, unaware of the Munras family, Maria Raine, Thomas Williamson, or the person of a short life under the strange square of sandstone.

THE VOLUNTEER

Private Kreiger, thin-faced, thin-bodied, stopped two paces before me and announced, "The lieutenant wants to see you. It's very important. You better get over there right away."

Any other soldier passing on the order would have called out, "The C. O. wants to see you." Then I would have known I had to report immediately. But that wasn't Kreiger's way. The words with his emphasis became an admonishment, almost his personal command. I knew he wouldn't leave until I acknowledged his message. He was conscientious and also shy, serious, and pathetic all in the same instant. Just looking at him standing in his loosely-fitted fatigues could make the G. I.s snicker. I held my face to a half-disguised smirk and replied, "Sure, don't worry. I'll be there in a minute." He was pleased. Once more he had carried out his duty fully.

If there was ever a man unsuited to be a soldier, it was Kreiger. I didn't know Private Kreiger any better than any other soldier. I never knew his first name then, but of the multitude of men I met at Fort Ord and in the Far East Command even after sixty years he was the most memorable. There was one reason. He was an example of the ongoing problem which most armies have: maintaining their numbers, "keeping up to full strength," as the military jargon terms it. They take whatever the levies yield, and try their damnedest to keep them. Private Kreiger at a slight 120 pounds with meager chest, pallid face, and broomstick arms was obviously not ideal soldier material. Added to those poor features, wouldn't you know it, he had a lazy left eye. When speaking to him it was a toss up as to which eye was making contact. A lazy eye? As I said they would take anyone and they did. An army barber had zipped most of the hair off his skull; and the remaining patch on top, a quarter of an inch long, was at best guess a mousey gray color.

On his arrival at Headquarters Company it was a given he would be poorly matched to any reconnaissance patrols or sapper duty; a place had to be found for him. By default and as no surprise to anyone he was assigned as a company factotum to run errands, to herd four or five Korean laborers around to load and unload trucks and dig latrines.

By a standing order a soldier's weapon had to be within reach at all times whether sleeping, in the chow line, at work, or sitting in the crapper. Throughout the day Kreiger's thin right shoulder sagged with the weight of a ten pound M-1 requiring him to hitch it up every two or three minutes.

It was notable, surprising how he quickly adjusted to his place in the company, never once complained of his lowly role, and always finished each task to the letter. Each message he carried was delivered in the manner of a child given great responsibility.

No humor, no gripes, no typical G. I. bullshit, or profanity ever filled his speech which was a sharp contrast with the other men who used the gerund form of their favorite "F" verb as an adjective to describe any person, place, or thing, or whatever else that didn't fit those categories. They repeated their raunchy jokes and gibed at one another from the time they got up in the morning until after lights out.

No one ever saw Kreiger smile. At least no one in the company ever reported he did. He was humorless, sober, earnest in his approach to all about him, but always risible in his appearance as the living Sad Sack of the funny papers. Perhaps he was aware that his wrinkled uniform hanging on his thin frame and his naiveté made him the butt of jokes; yet if he realized it he never gave the least indication. If he hadn't been so serious, he would have simply appeared a little "goofy."

One day he announced he had put in for a transfer to a front line company to be an aid man. What a thought. His reason given was that he planned to enter medical school on his G. I. Bill and serving as an aid man was that much more experience, a leg up so to speak. When that bit of news went around the tents there were howls and sputtering laughs.

"I wonder if he can keep the oral and rectal thermometers in the right places," some soldier cracked. Another added, "What if he becomes a surgeon? With that cocked eye of his, the patient might find his asshole in his arm pit."

Such were the speculations around the camp for days. Kreiger's avowed goal to become a doctor afforded the company plenty of joke material and none of it was wasted. He was a goldmine of laughs when his slouchy walk and his concerned frowns were aped in variations. Kreiger didn't hear most of the gags, but the odd one he did hear he listened to with a puzzled expression and simply walked away. He wasn't bothered by them or the pettiness of his work and went about the company area leading his Koreans from job to job.

His transfer didn't come through. That was to be expected for he would have to be replaced, and no commander would allow a man even one so ill-sorted as Kreiger to slip away. Replacements were always slow in arriving. Sometimes they never arrived. Kreiger played his clever game of patience and persistence; and as each transfer was denied he filled out another. Such dedication must have paid off.

Our regiment dallied in reserve doing some half-hearted training and enjoying the hot, drowsy days of summer when one morning we were told to pack up and move to the front line. Amid the striking of tents and the loading of trucks no one noticed Kreiger's absence.

The Chinese knew when our regiment took over the opposing section before them. They seemed to know everything and took advantage of our mens' unfamiliarity with the ground. A few days later a critical outpost several hundred yards beyond our main line was shelled caving in its bunkers and ripping away the barbed wire. Our men thinned out by the shelling were driven off by a sudden attack. To retake and hold the hill, timbers and sand bags were needed to rebuild the bunkers. It fell to us, the sapper platoon, to pack the materials up as close as we could get them to the top of an adjoining ridge in preparation for the attack.

Each soldier carried a small timber on left shoulder and his rifle on his right shoulder. We urged the Korean laborers to carry two timbers since they weren't loaded down with a weapon and a full cartridge belt. Our 20 GI's and about 40 Koreans spread into a meandering line along the narrow road to the base of the hill. Days before, that road had been littered with the rubbish of an aborted counterattack: rockets, grenades, ration cans, radios, a burned-out tank and a line of stretchers.

Moving beyond the main line made the guts uneasy. They never sat right in the belly. Unless very hungry, I never ate the heavy food like sausage patties from the C-rations. You took a deep breath now and then and let it out slowly while listening for the hiss and whine of an incoming shell. Each soldier's eyes looked out from the shadow of his helmet and scanned the hillsides for any movement and the ground ahead for trip wires. A shell hole large enough to shelter a man was noted and not forgotten until the next was spotted ahead. Fresh holes were a sign of trouble.

It began to rain. That was a plus. It veiled us and wasn't a dead giveaway as an intentional smokescreen would have been. We hoped it wouldn't clear off. If we were seen, the Chinese mortar men would drop shells on the road spacing them a few yards apart, neatly following its curves. Anyway it was a warm rain, and with all our gear and flak vests on we were wet but not cold.

We arrived with our first loads and found the men posted on the lower ridge sullenly dipping the rainwater out of their fox holes with empty ration cans.

Weeks before we took over the line, the main hill had been pounded with thousands of mortar and artillery shells blasting and churning the wet soil over and over. There were no bushes or grasses remaining on the top or half way down the sides of it. The branches of every tree had been sliced off by whining shrapnel leaving only a few splintered trunks with stump limbs on them. By its appearance the outpost was named Baldy, and in the heavy overcast and slow rain it was a close match to the scene of the horrors of Passchendale in 1917.

At the end of the day we dropped our last loads of sandbags and rolls of barbed wire on the ridge and returned to the supply bunker at the base of the hill. By then it was dark. That meant we had to remain there. Back at the main line a tank always rolled into position blocking the road at night. It and a platoon of men prevented any passage there. In the dark they accepted no password; any sound from the direction of the enemy drew bursts of machine gun fire. Tankers had a lot of ammo and they happily sprayed bursts at any noise they heard in front of them. In the morning they would discover if they had riddled anything be it the enemy or a stray cat.

The ground to the east and west of the supply point bunker was undefended, open to Chinese patrols.

With thick clouds overhead the night was total blackness. The rain tapped lightly on our helmets while we moved about with hands probing before us, feeling our way as mere blind men. No more could be seen with the eyes open than with them closed except for the faint and very distant glow of flares in the overcast fifteen or twenty minutes apart. The sporadic chunk-chunk-chunk of machine gun fire came alternately from the right and the left on the main line. There was no other way to pass the night stuck halfway between the main line and the outpost except to sit in or around the bunker in the darkness and listen for the noise of any movement.

After two hours in the dark, we heard voices approaching. I slid my finger forward and released the safety of my rifle. Tension was eased when word was passed along that Charlie Company was going up to make an assault on the main part of the hill.

"Grenades here, Get your grenades here," a soldier was offering in a low voice to enable the men to locate him. The squish and sucking of boots in the mud was made by the men of Charlie Company inching forward in the dark to find the man's hands passing out the little bombs.

"I don't need any. I'm the aid man," one soldier said.

Those words spoken with a slight lisp or slur were instantly familiar. The face that matched the voice flashed in my mind. "Kreiger," I asked, "is that you?"

"Yeah, who's that?"

"Roger, Headquarters Company. I see you made it."

"Yeah, this is my first time up on line. I'm the aid man now for C company."

"You're crazy for volunteering. You had it made at

Headquarters. Too many incoming rounds up there."

"It's what I want to do. I wouldn't change for anything."

The sound of his voice had been moving away as he went along with the line of men moving up the hill. In a few minutes they were all gone.

From far behind our lines came the deep thumps of artillery batteries firing. Seconds later a quartet of 105 shells streaked through the air overhead with their deadly rustling sound. A slight pause, then we heard the HARRUMPS! TNT blasted the earth on the far side of the hill.

A few minutes later a hiss like a steam leak came from high above, swiftly increasing in volume ...sssSSSHH! Everyone flattened on the mud. A split second later a flash of light and a shattering BLAM! Mortar fire! Surprise! Surprise! The Chinese were answering the challenge, lobbing their 82's over the hill and guessing the range and direction from a map. Fortunately, their estimate was slightly long and the shells landed on the opposite slope but still close enough to plink helmets with rocks and spent steel. A few rounds falling a bit short would have made hash of us. Before the forth round landed most men had rushed into the bunker

We could only huddle in there. The rain worked through the sandbags, between the logs of the roof and constantly dripped on us. It was too crowded to lie down leaving us only the option of sitting up. By gripping our upright rifles and resting our heads on our forearms we could doze a few minutes until cold water trickled from the back edge of our helmets and ran down our necks to waken us again and again. A soldier dozed off and fell against another man. There were coughs and snores in the blackness of the bunker. It was going to be a long night.

At about two o'clock a soldier poked his head in and announced, "We brought a casualty off the hill; we need two men to take him into the aid station from here."

"You can't get past the check point," someone protested, "You know that. Those tankers will riddle you."

"Leave him here," another voice said. "That's all you can do."

At the first gray light we left the bunker. There was no litter, no casualty to be seen. Others sitting outside had taken the man to the aid station.

We, plastered with mud and soaking wet, sloshed back toward the main line through the ruts cut in the road by the tracked vehicles and flooded with rainwater. The Koreans had to be urged on, to move faster and not to bunch up. Such a target seen through a lessening rain might tempt the enemy to lob a few more 82's.

The grapevine of the Army in Korea was amazing

in its speed and accuracy. It had the straight and skinny 99 percent of the time about what was happening along the line and outposts. By it we learned that the man on the litter was Kreiger. He was already dead when they started off the hill with him. He had been sitting at the doorway of a bunker with his flak vest unzipped when a shell hit nearby driving a fragment of steel into the center of his thin body. Kreiger's service on the hill as a medic lasted all of five or six hours. There was something sadder than usual about his death for he had never been the typical G. I. joking, swearing, and griping about the food and unpopular orders. He had borne all without a single complaint seemingly impervious to annoyance. Perhaps he comprehended far more than we realized.

The grapevine also had rumor but a less dependable one that went around Headquarters Company a week after he left. It surmised he was a survivor of a concentration camp. He would have been thirteen or fourteen years old in 1944 or 1945. The men of our company could have believed the tale because they had watched Kreiger walk about, the thin, pale soldier who yielded no smiles.

In our memories his comedic look faded away; and the jokes remembered, regretted lost their humor. He was granted his dignity of death.

In the Korean War records on line, I found his full

name was Gunther Hauptman Kreiger, not a Jewish one; but that was neither here nor there. Names meant little. He was no different than we were, and he had his dreams. He had patiently dealt with each day as it came and died like all soldiers die, in the dark, in the light, in mud and filth with a voiceless cry for life. You may think of his death as the cessation of a heartbeat or as another life not lived added to those on the litters shrouded with ponchos at the aid station. What is it to be remembered, remembered well, in place of a life lived?

CLYDE

Stubbornness may leave its mark on a face in the set of the jaw, and from age and disaffections that set may tense to a clench of the teeth paired with a mouth that turns down. Clyde's jaw though retained its relaxed line, but in middle age stubbornness came to show in his eyes by of loss shine and a slight recession. When his hair began to gray a sullenness and an obstinacy were detectable even behind the filmed surface of his glasses.

He had worn the same pair for years, and though he wiped them with his blue bandana they retained a slightly oily sheen from a mix of perspiration and skin oil that edged its way onto the frames and lenses. He worked in the fields through the heat of the day; and at times when he rested for a minute and removed his glasses to clean them there was a green stain on each side of his nose where their base metal touched his skin.

Clyde's walk, a hard-worked peasant's stride, resulted from following the mule-drawn cultivator for hours. Even when not driving the mule out in the fields there was a stiffness to the pose of his head, the effect of holding it upright against the pull of the reins looped around his neck. In a sense he was a peasant one tied to the land with no concept of doing anything else. He had farmed as a boy for he was of a family, a unit, that farmed. Their thoughts each year were of what they might plant in the next months and what would be the prospects of those crops. Later he worked the land by necessity for he had learned little else: his total knowledge was farming. There was never a dollar earned as wages in his pocket as he would not and did not work for another man. To hire out and follow the orders of someone else was an alien idea. His life was always guided by rigid independence and old habits. It was a life which allowed little humor or pleasure only brief, minor diversions.

Fashions had affected his choice of clothes when he was a young man; but at about age thirty men's styles had become meaningless. Dress for market day was a cap, a clean shirt and trousers, and the last cardigan sweater he had acquired; but when out in the fields he wore whatever old pants or shirts at hand unmindful of their loose fit, tears, or stains. It was difficult to imagine him as a spare-bodied, smooth-faced young man in the 1920's dressed in "whites" to play tennis; and it was more of a stretch to remember he once had friends and known giggling, flat-breasted flapper girls whose warm looks flirted from beneath their cloche hats.

All of his "lady friends" as they were referred to in the

twenties and thirties had married more promising, more pliable men; and from middle life on he had little reason to leave the farm except on business errands.

He ate his bland food in near silence and slept in his small upstairs room. Each weekday morning he rose early to plow, plant, and irrigate the fields with his father. They dug out the bindweed, dusted for pests and blight, and made enough from their sales in a farmer's market to pay the taxes and bills. Each year they farmed and took little note of their graying hair and aging faces. Not once did they have a thought of a vacation. The only time not spent working the farm was Saturday, market day, and Sunday. Sunday was their half-forgotten nod to the Christian admonishment, a whole day given to sit in the house and read the newspapers and magazines subscribed to year after year from which their beliefs were dawn. None of Clyde's conservative tenets formed during the 1920's and well considered and salted were to be altered. He, his mother, and father framed their sentences and opinions from a never changing stable of words and phrases. Any curiosities were few and small.

With work and chores finished and supper dispatched, Clyde retreated to the cluttered living room, sat in his old chair, and clicked the radio on. It was a ritual never varied unless some new stamps he had ordered arrived in the mail; and if some did, not a frequent event, he brought out a heavy, blue volume one of four that were half-filled after many years of selecting and buying. He picked up each stamp with a long pair of tweezers, squinted at it, and if he found it to be the one ordered mounted it on its proper page without showing any interest in the issuing country. The Ivory Coast, Belgian Congo, and Manchukuo remained only names in an atlas to him.

I don't believe he had traveled more than a hundred miles from the farm. That farm, ten acres of rich bottom land, was worked cautiously even frugally with part of it always lying fallow.

Nothing was ever purchased new if there was any possibility of repairing a piece of machinery or a damaged tool. Clyde or his father tinkered with it in the barnyard patching or jury-rigging it until it would serve; but if the part were hopeless Clyde located a used one in town, bought it for a fraction of the cost of a new one, and was smugly pleased with the saving.

An old Case tractor Clyde drove slowly across their fields of fine, damp earth had large, sharp lugs bolted to the drive wheels; and it was kept in service by cannibalizing another Case far beyond repair. The machine chugged ahead within a swirl of seagulls continually flapping up from the last furrow turned, to escape the noisy tractor advancing on them. Then they banked around to alight on the newly inverted earth behind the plow. Each waddling bird, stark white against black clods rolled and slicked by the moldboard, dashed forward to squabble with others over each newly exposed worm or grub.

A weather-beaten Victorian house bounded the farmyard to the west, and on the east side was a low, sway-backed barn with walls decomposing at their lower ends resting on the earth. Out to the north edge of the plowed fields was the wagon once used to bring in the annual crop of hay. Its rusted ironwork slowly flaked away, and the wood of the bed split in the summer heat or swelled and rotted a little more each rainy season. Dirt and small seeds gathered in each crack produced nascent blades of grass after the first rains. Closer to the barnyard, sitting on blocks, was the stripped frame of a Model T truck. Between the truck frame and the barn were a portable forge and an anvil still used to make repairs on equipment.

Dense-leaved blue gum eucalypts on the south edge shaded the yard and muffled the sound of the few cars and airplanes. In the afternoon the sea wind added its whisperings. The litter from the trees, spent leaves, woody fruits, and peeling bark fell on everything on that side of the yard. An old spike harrow and a set of derelict discs along with boxes and crates were being covered creating dark, dry lairs black widow spiders found snug and protective. Winter rains increased the camphor-like scent from the trees, one more welcome than the smell of the mule's corral.

Preparation for market day began for Clyde's mother Friday afternoon when she went into the poultry yard. There she kept her chickens, her ducks, and one felonious goose that nipped buttocks whenever a back was turned. She walked slowly around and grabbed the chickens and ducks by the neck that were to be killed and dressed for Saturday morning.

The vegetable produce of the farm, the boxes and crates of sweet potatoes, beans, melons, cucumbers, and asparagus were loaded onto the truck that evening. Beets and carrots were tied in bunches with jute twine and hosed off to leave them clean and crisp for market. Tomatoes, though, were their best seller; and boxes of them judiciously picked by Grandfather always made up half the load. Clyde sometimes finished the loading in the evening. Two electric wires strung overhead from the house to the barn were held a foot apart at mid point by a wood batten, and fixed to the underside of the batten was a porcelain base. It held an old pear-shaped light bulb that had a little nib on its end. The night wind swayed the unfrosted globe and its steely light and alternate soft shadows moved back and forth across the truck and barn wall. Clyde and his mother started for the city long before any hint of daybreak Saturday morning. Their old Dodge truck rolled out of the drive and turned north.

The truck already 14 or 15 years old in 1943 looked much older as it hadn't received any care except for the engine and tires. The gray paint on the cab was badly oxidized and if rubbed left a chalky smudge on the finger, yet the truck served its purpose and chugged the thirteen miles to the city with its loads.

Saturday was the worst day of the week for me for I was the nephew and grandson thirteen years old and obliged to work in the market for eight hours waiting on carping customers who pinched the fruit and complained about high prices. It could just as well have been midnight when they stopped by my house to pick me up. It was still black outside. I felt I was being cheated of half my night's rest but climbed into the cab and quickly fell asleep sitting upright, not to wake until we arrived.

The Farmer's Market not in the choicest part of the city was simply corrugated metal stalls lining two adjoining sides of a block. The enclosure behind them was parking space for the small-time farmers' trucks and cars. A few empty bottles were lying in the stall when we arrived, evidence of its use as a refuge at night where derelicts drank their wine unseen and passed into welcomed oblivion.

"We raise a non-acid," Clyde told the customers. "It's

a combination of the soil and our water that makes them so sweet." He repeated those words without variation any time he was asked why they had such a good taste. The tomatoes were simply vine-ripened and picked the day before. It wasn't just salesmanship though. He believed he had a way to raise a more flavorful product for their irrigation water, pumped from a shallow well, bore a peculiar metallic taste. Tomatoes from other fields tasted as sweet if left on the plant and harvested only when fully ripe.

"We raise a non-acid tomato," he stated to the potential customers standing before our stall and held out one in his hand to display the smooth, faultless skin and deep red color. It, resting in his curled fingers, contrasted with his cracked and stained skin and appeared even choicer.

"It's a combination of the soil and our water that makes them so sweet," he repeated many times until the end of the market day.

Clyde roped down the empty crates and boxes loaded on the truck and snapped the padlocks on the cabinets that held the scale and paper bags. We climbed aboard. Clyde started the engine and eased the old Dodge out onto the empty street. The sun was setting and we were on our way home after a tiring day. I knew each street we passed, each turn, stop sign, and traffic light on the way. We went by the huge, black gas tanks at the utility company, the dust collector at the lumberyard and then crossed over the railroad tracks that led into the Santa Fe yards.

The odd landmark that always puzzled me came at the next turn. It was the egg co-operative, a two story building with one of its gable ends facing the street we were traveling. A large white egg was painted on the black gable. "I'm a good egg," was the motto lettered in scrip above the stark illustration of the egg; yet those words were at odds with expression on the face of the egg. The corners of its mouth turned up in an unctuous smile; and the eyebrows dipped over the bridge of the nose, then arched high over the eyes. It bothered me. If it were a good egg, it shouldn't have such a devilish leer. Every time we passed that corner, I looked up to see that its expression hadn't changed and read the words again that declared it was a good egg.

The sky above was dimming to a darker hue, but the horizon was still light, a shade of mauve.

Grandmother sitting between Clyde and me nodded off. She weighed less than 95 pounds and with a spine bent into a dowagers hump was unable to stand fully erect. On the farm she shuffled about doing her chores: watering and feeding the poultry, all the while singing a near tuneless hymn. It seemed to be the same phrase repeated as if she had forgotten the words that should follow. For the occasion of market day she had rubbed an absurd patch of rouge on each wrinkled cheek, her sole concession to the new age. Her faded red hat, worn low on her head to cover her thinning hair, was at least ten years out of fashion. Suddenly she jerked up awake and stared unseeing at the street we were traveling.

A big orange moon on our left moved with us as we rumbled along. Dark trees and power poles darted between us and that October moon low on the horizon and rich with color. I watched the ball, and thought it watched me.

Grandmother and grandfather were children during the financial panic of 1888, and years later, when married, the memory of it prompted them to buy the farm as a hedge against another bust of the economy. Hard times became a fixture in their minds dictating their cautious farming. The 1929 crash though was far deeper and longer than any one of a gloomy set of mind could imagine. It never seemed to end, and they found what crops they raised difficult to sell. Despite that they were far better off than the migrants who had flowed into California begging for work at almost any wage.

Clyde suddenly turned the wheel of the truck to the left across the opposing lane and rolled onto a narrow, rough draft of a road between bare fields. We followed it for a hundred yards to its end in front of a small clapboard house standing alone. There were no trees or shrubs to give the house some relation to the earth. Any auto tires, garden tools, toys, boxes, or items of past and future use, any detritus of living was absent. The one frugal structure in the landscape had no full footing and rested on thin supports.

It puzzled me. We had never made a stop or even a slight detour before on our return home. I was annoyed and wanted us to be on our way for my legs ached from standing on the concrete floor all day.

Clyde stopped the truck and got out without saying a word. He walked to the door of the house and knocked. When it opened he stepped in.

Grandmother, still staring blankly ahead said flatly, "A woman he visits lives here."

I felt there should be a further explanation but none was given. She had speculated on Clyde's marriage prospects at times naming one or two local women; but now she simply sat there looking forward through the windshield.

The moon, which had seemingly followed us, had risen slightly higher from the horizon and paled from yellow to cold white. The finer details in the cab, the clutch, the brake, the gearshift were lost in the failing twilight. My shoes, somewhere on the floorboards, faded into the gloom. Thirty minutes later Clyde opened the door of the house and walked down the steps. He came towards the truck in his plugging stride and was followed by a woman in a plain, cotton dress. Uncle got into the truck and closed the door.

The woman stood by the open window and talked with Clyde about the high prices of food and rent and the prospect of winter rains. There were two small bruises on her left cheek and another on her right forearm, and she had made no attempt to give her straight hair a curl or even enliven its mousey color. There was not a speck of makeup on her face. She crossed her thin arms and held them against her body for warmth in the cool, fall air. In a few minutes she said goodbye and turned back toward the house.

I felt there was something not right about the woman for she never once looked at me, and no one mentioned her name. I couldn't remember ever seeing a woman as plain and meek as she was.

Uncle Clyde started the truck and turned it around to return to the highway. He drove with the headlights on for another 15 minutes, but they were dim and lighted the street poorly. The street lamp at each intersection approached first illuminated the gray hood of the old Dodge. After passing under the light, the shadow of the cab edged forward and the hood was again in darkness.

I was left off at my house. On the way up the drive I saw the moon had risen a little higher flooding the sky with its light. Only the brightest stars showed, and for some reason, they appeared farther from the earth. Empty fields about were a dreamscape.

Grandma and Clyde continued on to the farm a half mile away and most likely they found Grandfather benumbed by muscatel from his bottles hidden about the farm.

"BOOZE! BOOZING AGAIN!" Grandmother's grating voice would berate him as ever. His only defense was a listless silence.

Clyde had listened to the painful, repeated carping his entire life.

PART OF THE LANDSCAPE

*"In all this land there is only one girl for me
Her picture is on the dollar and her name is Liberty"*

That was the bit of doggeral I found chalked on the underside of a staircase in an old stage coach station many years ago. I had stopped on California's Highway 49 to explore that building constructed of unmortared fieldstone. Before such structures were deemed worthy of preservation and funds were found to restore them, they were left unfenced and open to be inspected by the idle and curious.

No signature was on the riser board as a claim of authorship, but it was dated 1933 and that recalled those very different times. The lines were probably written by some transient who had spent the night there, and those words were his message to the world and named the sole advantage of his life. That thought was also in the mindset of many Americans in that year and for many years afterward.

In 1933, I lived in California several hundred miles to the south of that station; and if you had looked to the southeast from our small house in that year or in any year of that decade, a heated layer of air would be shimmering over the mesa and the tracks and sleepers of a railroad. You might have seen a distant, dark speck in it shifting slightly left and right and up and down. The speck would grow in size as the minutes passed, become less fluid as it neared, and resolve into a human figure wading through a phantom lake. At the seam between the horizon and the pastel sky, slowly emerging details would reveal the figure as a hobo or one of the young men wandering the nation in a hopeful search for job.

They came one at a time, dressed in blue bib overalls and carrying a rope-bound bundle or a laundry bag over one shoulder. There within three miles of the Pacific Ocean it was hot; yet it was fifteen or twenty degrees cooler than the desert the man had passed through a day or two before. Many came that way. Sometimes one of the men stopped beside the rails, removed his sweat-stained hat, and wiped his face and neck with a kerchief. It was a rest that gave him much relief. Beneath his shoes the desiccated wood sleepers had cracks in the length of them; and any fragment of a broken bottle lying on the gravel ballast reflected a minute but intense glint of the sun. The man narrowed his eyes and peered across the fields of barley stubble and dry, hardened earth to the few houses scattered about. Next he would consider the distance he had yet to travel. If the man arrived in the evening, he turned aside into a small grove of Australian gum trees beside the railroad. There he spent the night and left the matted leaves of a temporary bed and the ashes of a fire. The fire was unneeded for warmth; but its flickering light was a companion and a declaration of his presence in that portion of the grove and a place on earth.

In the predawn glow of the morning he discovered our crank little house, solitary in a field on the far side of the dirt road; and half an hour later he watched the verge of the sun send taunt shadows of it, power poles, and fence posts spanning the fallow earth westward. Patiently he waited for what he considered the favorable moment to cross the empty field and knock on our back door. The back door was always the prudent choice for one would not presume to call at the front door of even so humble an address as ours when the purpose was to beg. Timing must have been considered a key element to his success: if too early or too late he might only receive a shake of the head. Once or twice a month one of those men stood, hat in hand, at the foot of our worn stoop and with his pride subdued by hunger asked if he could perform some chore for a small meal. Paint, rake the yard, or mend a fence: he would do anything. Our mother stood behind the rickety screen door and frowned doubtfully estimating if she could afford to feed him. A refusal was accepted with a quiet nod and added to all those the man had received in the past for each one knew the plight of others might be little better than his own. It was hard times and there were few who could afford to be openhanded. If he were fed he had to sit on a box in the back yard to eat a fried egg sandwich and the apple he was given.

On his trek to the West Coast, the massive mountains and the sweep of the great valleys through which he passed had reduced him to a mere speck moving across the land. The shining rails leading to their distant vanishing points ahead and behind him defined his separation from the inhabited world. Nightfall and a bed on the ground sharpened it. The next glow of morning light at the horizon would mark one more of the fifteen to twenty thousand awakenings left in his lifetime. No person, no people awaited his arrival in the near future. All that was ahead of him was the unknown, and the unknown was feared to be worse or hoped to be better each time he arrived in a new town or city.

Each man went on north to sleep in many other groves and in riverbank thickets along the Salinas, the San Joaquin, the Sacramento, the American, and the Mokelumne Rivers. They spread into California's farms and orchard lands where they walked the long, dusty roads to each succeeding harvest, earned a little money, or begged enough food to keep going. If there had been some assurance of their next meal, it might have been something of an adventure. Men in other places and times had sought their fortunes under far worse conditions; but for these wanders there was no El Dorado, no Cockaigne, no Big Rock Candy Mountain, no land of ease and plenty only endless pilgrimages to the rumored locations of work. In summer their only relief from the sun and wavering heat was under trees or at the shady side of a building. In the winter they sought shelter under bridges, in sheds and boxcars, or even beneath the eaves of warehouses. There they might sit and watch patiently for the rain to cease. Their evenings might be spent crowded around a campfire with others waiting for a can of stew to cook the ingredients of which had they not bought them they had begged or filched. They were drawn together by the fire and a discovered brotherhood of desperation. In that circle of wavering light they were reduced to mere faces. Many of them spoke their words in the twang of the Southern Plains. A few yards beyond their fire was a dimly lighted backdrop of willow leaves or the stalks of a cane brake. For days and even weeks they slept under starlight and moonlight and listened to the chirr of crickets, the croak of frogs, and the whine of pestering mosquitoes. For them liberty was the sole advantage of their lives.

At the beginning of the 1930's the American landscape

and thoughts were being shaped by the Great Depression. There had been panics and depressions before, but none of them had the breadth and the obstinacy of the one that spanned the entire decade. Everyone was baffled by the growing void of uncertainty; yet all the politicians had ideas, do this, do that to move the costive economy, or simply have faith and do nothing for prosperity, they avowed, was just around the corner.

Perhaps too much has been written about it by some. Economists were eager to define it as a period of "overproduction," a concept they had learned in class. It would have been more accurately labeled a period of under-consumption for people suffered and went hungry amid all the overproduction that awaited sale but they could not purchase. Certainly too little was written about those years by the multitudes, anxious and out-at-elbows, who lived through the decade and carefully counted the dimes, nickels, and pennies remaining in their pockets. The ones who suffered most did the least writing for they were scantly lettered for the most part, reticent, and bewildered by conditions they had no hope of altering.

Then too there was culpability in being poor and unemployed. Some people neither poor nor unemployed recited their opinion that the jobless had some defect of character and if they would just try harder they would have a job. The unemployed and hungry could only endure the sniffy looks and hope for better times.

After the Depression faded, most wanted to forget they had fallen into a shameful poverty whatever the cause. The war years blurred their recollections, and the peace years filled them with far pleasanter thoughts. There was a collective and understandable wish to ignore the despairs of the 1930's.

In that time my brother and I knew a dollar was hard to come by. We had been told that often enough. Save for a rare nickel we were given to buy an ice cream bar or a penny we might find in the dirt, we seldom saw money. When I started school though I had been given a quarter. That was enough to buy a loaf of bread and a quart of milk with a cent or two returned. It was a large coin in my small, smooth hand. On one side of it was stamped the figure of a woman standing by a wall, and on the reverse side was an eagle with its wings spread in flight. I carried the silver coin, tied securely in the corner of a bandana, to school. There I entered it into a savings account; and I was given a little, blue passbook wherein my twenty-five cents was recorded. It was a long time before any interest figured at rock bottom percentage appeared in the deposit column and even longer before the balance exceeded a dollar.

We had a vague idea that our father worked hard somewhere. He returned home in the evenings, sat slowly and heavily on his chair at the table, and spoke very little as he ate an unseasoned and uninspired meal.

We knew there was a chronic lack of money but did not perceive just how it affected us. At the beginning of the school year our faded bib overalls, patched and re-patched over the knees, were replaced by two new pairs plus two new shirts. We delighted in the smell of their factory-fresh cloth. There were shoes for each of us to wear when an occasion required them, a new pair for my older brother and his old ones Shinola-ed and perhaps half-soled for me. They were an option for most days and we enjoyed the freedom of bare feet summer or winter.

The grown-ups sat in the house on Sunday and spoke of the "hard times" and how things had never been so tight. The rest of their talk bored us so we ran outside to play. We being small boys living in a world hardly a mile and a half in scope were not aware of much that happened beyond our sight. We did not comprehend the labor strikes or the Red scares or the bother over the promises of the Ham and Eggers. Along the roads we spotted the red and gray yin yang signs labeled "Technocracy", and when we asked a question as to their meaning we were fobbed off with the answer that they had something to do with politics.

We twigged the stinted hopes of the migrants who wandered into our world from the sober faces of the men, the harried look of the women, and the attitudes of their children divided between the poles of shyness and boasting. Though they lived in tents, shacks, lice-ridden outbuildings and bore the odors of sweat and urine, we did not sense their condition as squalor. It was close, familiar to us and we did not perceive all of its meanings. They were the Okies, the Arkies, the outlanders, the rootless who moved now and again as far as their little mite of money allowed them. We owned a house and, though a frail one, it was a fixed place in the landscape and in our minds.

There was one sign and not words by which we understood the Depression. It was literally a sign nailed to a post in front of our house. We scanned the neat lettering, but could not yet read the longer words. It was explained to us that it said that a man lived there who did carpentry at reasonable rates. By that sign even unread we first began to grasp the lack of employment and the scarcity of money.

For the adults the Depression must have seemed interminable. There was a growing fear that it might never end. It went on for years with little change, and its louring uncertainty eroded any expectations of relief.

Time for us hardly appeared to pass at all but for different reasons and in different ways. All things within our sight seemed immutable and fixed in a never-ending present. The shapes of the smooth, brown mesas would stand unmarred at the edge of the mumbling Pacific never to bear a change. There were no new roads and no new structures to be built or even expected in our landscape. We had the dry, empty mesas to wander under a constant and benevolent sun, one which bleached our uncombed hair and tanned our shirtless backs. Our time out of school would be spent as each whim moved us. We could not imagine a distant future in which we would not be two small boys with few cares and no real wants. Yet by some conspiracy each year that passed nudged us nearer puberty. With each year a bit more awareness came and revealed the airiness of those beliefs.

The landscape, not a dramatic or picturesque one, lay along the Pacific Coast where a middling surf broke on the beach for most of the year. Each wave rose into translucent green before it tipped; then it collapsed from one end of the shore to the other like a closing seam and spread up the sand in wobbling froth.

Parallel to the beaches the land was dully flat, composed of long shelves crossed here and there by dry washes and narrow tidal inlets. It was mesa country. What caused it to be so marvelously level remained a mystery until years later when we learned that those strips of land were marine terraces planed flat by interglacial surfs when the sea had risen to different levels in the past million years. Sea shells and root casts could be found in road cuts and well diggings proving that the two or three visible terraces were not the only ones created. Beneath the hard, red soil of our yard were ancient beaches that had been formed, left stranded during the ice ages, and covered in later millenia.

Miles to the east beyond the terraces was the granite rubble of the Coast Range. Its crests traced an irregular horizon along the paled edge of the sky, and their crumpled slopes were covered with boulders nested in a velure of dark chaparral.

There was never enough rain to support more than a knee-high scrub, bits of cactus, and a few stunted oaks in the gullies. In the drought years, barley planted in the fields rose only a few inches before it headed out and dried. Rain in most winters was frugal and short-lived; but in a "good" year the wind brought the smell of rain before it was released from the lowering clouds. The first drops fell on the parched earth as a benefaction, an event more welcome than holidays. To feel them dotting the skin was to have a sense of renewal. They pelted the dust creating a scent familiar to us but a rare one unmatchable in any other time or place. In the wetter years storms left puddles on the dense earth reflecting a fresh, clearing sky and its fragmented clouds.

We waited for the first minute spears of grass to rise

by magic from the softened ground, grow, and spread a fugitive green over empty fields and along the roadsides. First to sprout were the filaree, foxtail, and oats and then came the other beggar weeds of Southern California: cheese weed, burr clover, pineapple weed, and lastly the thistle. Hazes of yellow mustard blossoms hovered lightly on the slopes and fields favoring certain swathes and the ragged margins near fences. The patches of green masking the red earth were enjoyable; but they never lasted long enough for us to be sated with that color, the pledge of the plant world. The long dry season would come all too soon. Our land was poorly favored. We wished for some miraculous change in the climate that would bring more rain and keep the soil damp to nurture grass the year round. As winter ended the wild oat stems lengthened, paled to gold, and nodded their seed heads in the west wind to shell out implicit generations. For a few days or a week the hay-like odor of the drying grasses drifted in the warm air. Through the remainder of the year the dead stalks weathered in the sun and fog to a silvery gray. Nothing would be notable in the dry season except the June bugs who announced the arrival of their month by mindlessly butting against lighted windows at night.

By looking at the landscape with half-closed eyes and discounting the buildings, power poles, and exotic trees the country could be imagined as it was when Father Serra first crossed it, one of unmarked hillsides and sweeps of level land. In the Mexican Era, before wells were dug and roads were cut into the mesas, it was a featureless grazing land. Languid cattle and durable goats had wandered on the unfenced expanses and beat dusty paths through its sere weeds and brittle scrub. Ground squirrels had scurried onto bare mounds and froze upright before diving into their burrows. It was a forgotten place, parched, sleepy, event-less, of little potential in those years before the railroad came and time was so finely and preciously divided by Yankee needs. Windmills appeared on the skyline prior to the turn of the century and water from shallow wells was raised and flowed in the irrigation ditches of farms and orchards. Most of the farms were small; and except for the orchards there was no single cash crop, no economies of scale. In later years the less successful farmers were forced to sell all or part of their land. The people who bought the bits of acreage and lots built houses on them in a haphazard way. Hence the old farmhouses remained nested in established trees and bushes with their once-whitewashed barns and sheds snuggled about them while a hundred yards away one or two jerrybuilt bungalows were raised on untilled fields. Small, flyspecked stores and gas stations were sited at the busier crossroads giving the landscape a look of semi-rurality, a place held in mid-step between farming and urban sprawl by the Depression. If it ever had an engaging aspect, it was two centuries before when it was still empty of roads and buildings and wore the simplicity and cleanliness of a desert.

Cocks crowed at dawn from all directions. Cows mooed and chickens cawed indolently in the midday heat, drawn out calls in a timeless, sun-beaten country. Those country sounds came not only from the old farms but also from the backyards of the newer houses whose tenants kept livestock and poultry to provide themselves with milk and eggs and the odd chicken diner.

The decrepit fences harboring their line of weeds and the unused fields were ours by default. What the owners had abandoned, we might claim and will to be what we wished. We explored, savored the untenanted barns and stock pens and conceived them to be the scenes of great adventures yet to be lived. We possessed it all with our imaginations. By tying bandanas around our necks, we were instantly cowboys; and the next day the bandanas were our headgear and we became pirates on some nameless sea.

If play palled in our long, sunny days we examined the fence posts, ditches, and gopher holes. There were leaves and spider webs to be studied. We watched every bug found and poked it to see what it would do.

Even barbed wire, and rusting iron were worth our inspection. For many minutes of each day the landscape was recommitted to memory. The distant stands of gum trees were always there inviting us into their scented and shaded naves.

The house we had lived in for years would be called a shanty and a curiosity if it still existed today. Its walls had been framed up and covered with wide boards mounted vertically. Then battens were nailed over the cracks where each met. Total cost: about a hundred and fifty dollars. The exterior of the cramped, three-room house remained unpainted and warped and split in the sun. Dashes of rain in winter darkened the walls to a charcoal gray and leached rust stains from nail heads into the wood. Only up under the eaves where the effects of sunlight and water could not reach did the lumber retain any of its original color. The structure was built on a piece of leased land at the beginning of the Depression. A few years later our father managed to buy two acres that were part of an unworked farm. Furrows plowed into the soil years before, then covered by grasses and hardened by summer heat were remnants of its former use. He sawed the house in half, mounted one section at a time on a set of old wagon wheels, and towed it across the highway to the new property. The move was made surreptitiously in the middle of the night to avoid posting a bond required by the State when crossing the highway. The halves were set up on scantling supports and rejoined; but the house remained singular and naked in that empty field despite the effort to tie it to the earth with a few bushes at its front and sides. The plants did not thrive in the dense soil and bear sufficient foliage to cover the gap between the lower edge of the walls and the ground. The house rested in the field attached to the scene around it by two thin wires from a power pole. A passerby might have supposed it had been abandoned.

Early on summer mornings the rays of the sun drove out the moisture absorbed by the wood at night causing the siding of the east wall to creak. The sounds awakened us. Beams of bright light entered the small kitchen window, passed through an open doorway, and slanted across the dim void of the bedroom. It was too early to stir about. Our parents were still asleep. We could only sit quietly in our beds and watch the motes of dust as they suddenly appeared floating up out of the darkness into the shafts of light. Slow air currents moved them about in gyres, and they winked out when they rolled from the path of the sun's rays.

Dust entered the house around its worn doors and though the cracks in the lumber of its walls. The road at the front of the house was unpaved, and each car that passed pulled a rolling dust cloud in its wake. It drifted off the road and coated the walls and windows of the house and fence posts. A khaki layer was even detectable on the rusted strands of barbed wire. A few times each year the county sent a tank truck out to dribble water on the road to lay the powdered earth; but it was never often enough for any good so we suffered the dust until the road was paved. Then it became known as the "street", though it was a county road that passed more empty fields than homes.

We accepted the house and the smelly privy that was stationed at back of it. There were larger and better houses to be seen: some properly sided with planed lumber, some stucco-ed, and all painted. There was no question why we didn't live in one of those other homes. We assumed without the least thought that they were for other people. Our house though small and flimsily built was a reliable shelter. So it proved to be on a rare winter night when the wind moaned around its corners and it creaked like an old ship under sail. The electricity failed. Father brought out the kerosene lamp and lighted its wide wick. He replaced the chimney and set the implement on the center of the worn oilcloth that covered the kitchen table. All of us sat within the glow of the yellow flame, motionless within the clean glass, and listened to the dash of raindrops against the windows.

We could not conceive how the house, the food

given us, the beds slept in, the clothes worn could be any different. Such was a life in which we were only spectators who surveyed the land about us and did not expect the least change. What ever would cause it be altered? Bright imaginings at play did not extend to reality.

The setting autumn sun with its rays at their lowest angle ambered the railroad embankment and fence posts in those minutes too short-lived to suit us. The few trees along the western skyline darkened into lacy, black silhouettes against an orange horizon. Opposite the trees the haze over the mountains was given a rose blush. The yard and the surrounding fields became less familiar and more intriguing as shadows gradually filled in the low ground.

We hid from each other in the darkening places and behind bushes, panting, listening to our thumping hearts in anticipation of being found. Being discovered was the cue to dash off in a weaving chase through the grass. It was exhausting play and truces had to be called while we stood bent over with hands on knees, gasping for air.

The houses and trees seemed more distant as the turn of the earth rounded off the last glow of the day. Lights appeared as the darkness edged higher. The moving lights were on autos traveling along the narrow highway, and the fixed ones marked a few illuminated windows and porch lights. They varied from white to pale yellow to the small, red taillights. All were gathered in a skimpy, broken line of a half circle. Moonrise turned the landscape into one known by its details, but unfamiliar in its whole aspect. Fields nearby were frosted with an argent light, and the hills beyond were reduced to black shapes devoid of any detectable feature. Under the gauzy emanation filling the dome of the sky the mountains became pale borders of the farthest horizon. The moonlight descended on our heads, shoulders, and bare arms; yet it left our eyes indistinct in shadows. The grove of eucalypts across the road became a jet mass, silent in the breathless air. There in the aisles between the trees, the earth was covered with a litter of leaves and shed bark; and they in turn were mottled into patterns of moonlight and shadow. We were poised to go farther in, walk on the crunching leaves and pass through the scattered shafts of numinous light; but mother's voice called our names from the back door of the house. We were loath to leave this new country steeped in the fragmented beams of the moon.

"Just a half hour more. Plee...ese, just a few minutes to play."

Such requests were bootless; and we were obliged to leave the newly discovered province which exhaled a mood of expectancy, a promise of adventure. In our slow pacing toward the house, the earth was warm and comfortable beneath our bare feet.

Under that moon the fields could become what we wished, but we were never quite sure what they should be. The edge of a mesa might turn into a sand dune and a camel train might appear on its crest with a coffle of slaves following. It could be the shore of an unknown island ready for our exploring eyes. All imagined exotic worlds of brigands and sailors would fade with the first gray light of day and leave only our daytime scene.

The house was hotter than the night air outside. We spread-eagled on the cool, white cotton of our beds; but the pillows and sheets warmed quickly. We shifted and tossed to find cooler places to rest arms and faces.

An indirect light spilled from the kitchen and illuminated the knots and water stains on the exposed roof sheathing above us. When stared at our fanciful imaginations joined them into grotesque faces and animal shapes. After attempting to sleep and then opening the eyes again, the creations were still there staring down at us. They could not be dismantled into mere stains and knots. The familiar outlines of the beds, the bureau, and a chest were now only shapes in dark gray and charcoal. Some nameless thing behind them might be expected to rise up and reveal itself, but nothing ever did. All remained inanimate, solidly fixed.

The ticking of the alarm clock instead of measuring the passage of time seemed to expand it. Darkness became interminable. Mind and body were keyed up, not ready for rest. Unintelligible whispers of the grown-ups came from the kitchen, their voices hushed to avoid waking us from a presumed sleep. A car passed on the road out front; and a vertical strip of light from its headlamps slipped through a gap in the curtains, flashed onto the far wall, and moved swiftly across it.

We were separated from the night outside by no more than inch-thick boards and were always aware of noises near and far. A cricket chirred. A cow lowed in the distance and became quiet again. A while later a dog started barking. It too was far from the house and its call muffled, less canine. The night was known better then, of how the rain of moonlight outside lifted the familiar into the fabled.

On moonless nights when the curtains were pulled aside, a wealth of stars was visible winking in a broken, auspicial rhythm. A covert message was in the brighter points of light, secrets to be revealed to us in some future time. We lay our heads on our pillows again and without any drowsing prelude fell asleep. The little house, the earth turned beneath the dusting of minute lights distant beyond our comprehension. Night had spoken to us.

The railroad came out of Mexico, crossed the mesa, and went on north to the city thirteen miles away. Its rails divided the landscape with the portion on the west bordering the ocean and that on the opposite side, the remainder that met the hills to the east. The railroad itself was another diversion. Learning to walk on a single rail was tricky, and we never got the hang of it to go very far without touching a foot on a wooden tie to regain our balance. On hot days it was the heat of the steel on our bare feet that forced us to give up even sooner and hop onto the gravel.

The old locomotives that loomed in the distance and then went click-clacking along those tracks were the most powerful things within our ken. Like all boys before us, we were awed by the black smoke puffing from the stack and the steam jetting from the pistons. The big driving wheels and the massive linkage were fascinating to watch as they drove the train forward. Play paused when the whistle was heard in the distance; then it was time to count the boxcars and tank cars that clattered north or south. On the sides of the rolling stock were names that always drew rapt attention when we learned to read: the Southern Pacific, Burlington, Santa Fe, Great Northern, Union Pacific, the Keystone Route, and the Central Pacific. The cars had been gathered from all over America to rumble past the little house. The rest of our country was not a fiction. There passing was the evidence that it existed far beyond the mountains. If we had hungered for anything, it was to be over the hills and far away to see the origins of those wonderful names. We stood in an unfenced field below the curving embankment and waved to the engineer and the brakeman. They never failed to return the greeting with a slowly waved hand for the two small boys standing in the expanse of barley stubble and dry, red earth.

The passenger coaches were painted an olive drab and had squat, gold lettering on their sides that named the company that owned them. They were dirty cars with rust streaks leached down their sides. At night, the light from their grimy windows rippled along the edges of the fields. A few passengers inside sat reading their newspapers, oblivious of the countryside hidden in the darkness.

The tracks were little more than a hundred yards from the house; and during hot, drowsy days the wails of the steam whistle became the auditory motif of home. In the darkness and under the twinkling of stars on chill nights, the calls entered through the rough lumber of the walls. The wavering blasts were familiar and homely as the clucking of chickens. We parsed those warnings, noted their changes of pitch. They rolled toward us in a nasal howl; then dropped as the engine passed the house. In drawing away the sounds became lower and mellower and mixed with the clanging of the bell and the metrical clicks of the wheels. They echoed in the distance as a farewell from the great, black machine leading its pennon of smoke far into the darkness, into memory, and into legend. Then silence. Slowly, the noises of the countryside reclaimed the night again.

Sunday in those years was truly a day of rest. Stores closed for the day. Working men with jobs slept late; and when they awoke they shaved and dressed in clean clothes. From the open doors of their houses they savored their twenty-four hour reprieve from labor. They leaned against the doorjambs, smoked, and viewed the state of their yards noting any successes or failures.

At mid-morning the bell of the church swung high on its yoke. The man who pulled the rope pulled it with a will, with devout purpose; and the plangent notes of its iron rolled out unhindered across the fields their timbre fluctuating as the mouth faced the listener and then away. That insistent clangor announced the impending services to be held in a white, wood-framed church of a Protestant rigor. The congregation that arrived in a platoon of black cars, dusty in the summer and mud-splattered in winter, had all put on a benign face with their Sunday clothes. They were the farmers, mechanics, and housewives of the country; and on that day their smiles for their neighbors were broader and more readily given. They all ascended the steps of the church, the men nodding self-conscious hellos and their women clucking, all-smiling. They came together to practice an odd religion. Their god was not a fearsome, vengeful one; nor was he one who gave unlimited forbearance. Their Christ and the Apostles seemed no more corporeal than the cardboard cutouts placed around the crèche at Christmastime.

Gravure pictures of the Holy Family were shown to us. The artist had depicted them staring heavenward, the essence of purity, bloodless, devoid of any earthly desire; but they appeared simply fey. The preacher spoke and once or twice even ranted of hell; yet it wasn't the palpable, horrific hell in the paintings of Bosch or Grunewald. It was a theoretical hell undefined and located in parts unknown. Their heaven was equally vague. No one explained heaven to our satisfaction. What, we wondered, could be so desirable and yet not describable in terms known to us. If we had to be good boys to achieve it, we should have a good idea what it was all about. We were not aware of church dogmas or a long calendar of holy events to be faithfully observed. There were readings from the Bible, talks on the Bible, Bible stories, Bible classes, chapbooks, and hymnbooks. The religion appeared to be dependent on the printing press. We sat reverently as we were able and toyed with our buttons or stared at the thinning white hair and liver-spotted skins of the ancients who sat around us. They were old, the church was old. The heavy pews and the quartersawn oak paneling on the walls betokened sterile, dusty age to us. The words that were spoken from the pulpit were uttered in a joyless drone. We couldn't conceive just what it all was intended to mean for us.

At the conclusion of the services the congregation perhaps bored by the sermon yet feeling all the better for hearing it exited into the glaring sunlight and brighter colors. Since it was Sunday and the women were hatted and dressed in prints and the men were suited and tied, they went visiting. That was an acceptable thing to do; that or sit in the parlor, read the paper, and listen to the radio. There was segregation by gender. The women entered the homes of the people visited for tongue-clicking gossip. Menfolk (the term was still in use then) usually remained outside and talked while they divided their attention between each others' faces and the ground at their feet. The men leaned against their cars and rested one foot on a running board. On warm days, ties were loosened and coats removed. They nudged their hats back a little and revealed pale foreheads. Their freshly-shaven faces were those of hard-worked men, and their tanned lower halves appeared even darker in contrast with their white shirts. Talk was slow and predictable, more of an amenity than communication. One of them made a statement and the others slowly nodded assents as if it were a truth agreed on beforehand.

The family income slowly increased, and at the end of the thirties father started to build a new house a bit at a time as enough money was saved to buy the materials. It was solidly constructed of cinder blocks and was to have a bathtub and a flush toilet. While the new home was being built; the old one was being dismantled. Its warped boards were pulled loose and nailed down in the new house for sub flooring and its studs used to build partitions. Even the scraps were gathered and stacked for firewood. The old house was used up. Little of it remained except some bent nails and a pile of red, mineralized roofing paper.

Plein Air artists were drawn to Southern California in the four decades before World War II and were bemused by those portions of it not cluttered or staked out into lots and hawked with much hoopla by promoters. The painters ignored the haphazard development and pictured on their canvases what pleased them most: mountains blued by distance and poppied hillsides. Clusters of oak and Eucalyptus trees were fitted into their Arcadias. The paled colors of many landscapes were a nod by the artist to the dominant sunlight. In part their idyllic pictures encouraged an influx of sun worshipers and health seekers. They were almost too late for their chosen scenes were being encroached by development and income property as they painted. Arcadias in the modern age cannot last, even less favored, frugal ones. Time and greed works against them. Some painters understood the end of an era was approaching and painted the fleeting nature of that life before crowding and the automobile erased it.

The landscape eventually mutated into suburbia. No longer a place in an era, its past quality was hinted at in those paintings, in photos, and recollections.

A return made thirty years later occurred by chance. I had been on an errand driving along a new freeway when on my right I recognized the old railroad embankment. At the first ramp I turned off and looked about. There was the old landscape with its stand of gum trees and the edge of the mesa. All the roads were now paved. I had, by simple chance, parked on "the street" in front of the lot on which the old shanty and the new house in turn had rested. The new house was missing. Its concrete footings had been rooted up and the site smoothed over by a bulldozer. Part of the barley field to the west of the lot had been sliced away to create an underpass. An old hedge, thrusting out branches and pursuing primal shapes, was the only evidence that a house had once stood there. Apartment buildings and a gas station now covered some of the fields.

Around the new structures young men talked or worked on cars. Young women fussed with small children and laundry. The changes were to be expected, inevitable in that time and place. The fields had been filled with buildings and confined at their edges with pavement. I watched the young men and women. Did they have their own landscapes gathered when they had walked the lanes and back roads in some other country?

Those young people would never hear or see what we had witnessed in the heat ripple on those sparsely peopled mesas decades before. In an earlier time could each have once walked on a divergent road and a lifetime later, in a recollection, see himself in that landscape?

If they could have seen us as we were then, shantied by the railroad, they would have said we had lived in poverty; but we could not have believed it and certainly would have denied it. We never felt deprived. Poverty was relative. Everyone had lived from paycheck to paycheck when there were paychecks and managed somehow when for months, years there were none. Though all cash including small change was spent with much care, we always had enough to eat even if it was hash made with penny-a-pound potatoes and tinned government beef.

In our unsullied optimism we had doubted nothing, feared nothing. After measles we suffered only lesser ailments and always felt a boundless energy and strength in our small bodies. To our young senses there was a clarity and freshness to each sound heard and image witnessed; and we hopefully viewed the hills, houses, and trees in the shifting lights and shadows the sun created as it rose and moved westward. Overhead were the singing notes of the power lines and at times the lazy drone of an airplane lost high in the clear sky. We ignored our patched and faded clothes and had dashed with fervor across the stubble fields, our thin legs driving like pistons. To breathe sweet air and explore our world while at loose ends and easy in mind, had been a delight.

The parched, rag tag landscape had been the remnant fields beyond the city, but now they were. paved and urbanized. Yet, it had once been wholly ours where we had listened in the darkness for the crickets' chirps and the few barks and lowings. The chuffing train with its insistent bell had sped into the distance; and its whistle blasts had rolled across the mesa returning in hollow, fading echoes.

****

We had been part of our landscape from which we perceived direction; and we still held vestiges of our lives spent in that time and place. Only once would we lark in sunlit days and feel the warm earth under foot. Only once would the stars and the sounds of the night have untold meanings.

Made in the USA
San Bernardino, CA
07 November 2015